COO

FOR

PLEASURE

SUE LAWRENCE

CONTENTS

Published exclusively for J Sainsbury plc
Stamford House Stamford Street
London SE1 9LL
by Martin Books
Simon & Schuster Consumer Group
Grafton House 64 Maids Causeway
Cambridge CB5 8DD

ISBN 0 85941 842 1

First published 1993
Second impression October 1993

Printed in Italy by Printer Trento

THE AUTHOR

Sue Lawrence grew up in Edinburgh, before studying French at Dundee University. She developed a passion for French food during periods of living in France. Her culinary experience was broadened by travelling and living abroad.

In 1990 she won *The Sunday Times Scotland Amateur Chef of the Year*, closely followed by *BBC Masterchef* in 1991. Sue lives in Cramond, near Edinburgh, with her husband Patrick and their three children. She specialises in cookery writing and demonstrating.

Pictured on the front cover: Arbroath Smokie Salade Niçoise (page 30)
Pictured on the back cover: Salmon fillet with Basil Cream Sauce (page 60)

Double Tomato Tarts

*Pheasant Breast with
Mango Sauce*

Mile-High Ice Cream Pie

All recipes in this book give ingredients in both metric (g, ml, etc.) and Imperial (oz, pints, etc.) measures. Use either set of quantities, but not both, in any one recipe.

All teaspoons and tablespoons are level, unless otherwise stated. 1 teaspoon = a 5 ml spoon; 1 tablespoon = a 15 ml spoon.

Egg size is medium (size 3), unless otherwise stated.

Vegetables are medium-size, unless otherwise stated.

Freshly ground black pepper should be used for pepper throughout.

INTRODUCTION

The recipes in this book reflect my love of cooking; a love which has been influenced greatly by travel. I was brought up on wholesome, but plain, Scottish fare, and it was only when I started living abroad that my culinary outlook widened. The different cooking methods of various nations have always interested me, and so by watching, by practising and, most of all, by enjoying food, I have learned to cook. For me, the greatest pleasure is to have both exquisite food and excellent company; the whole concept of conviviality revolves around lively conversation and the communal enjoyment of the meal. So a simple salad or bread and cheese or a bowl of soup – with the right company – can be as memorable as a punitively expensive dinner in a well-known restaurant. The purpose of this book, however, is to produce dishes that stand on their own; riveting companions are an optional extra! Simplicity is the hallmark of these recipes, which are designed to enhance the natural taste of the ingredients by the use of complementary flavours. The added advantage of such a simple approach to cooking is that, when you have guests, you are not left out in the kitchen fretting over complicated recipes.

In the last decade there has been a boom in the variety of food available in the supermarkets. It seems there is scarcely an ingredient in the world that is not stocked in the larger stores. Certainly that is the impression I have had when returning to the UK from periods spent living abroad. I found I could recreate my favourite dishes from other countries quite easily. But by doing so I was ignoring some of the wonderful dishes of my youth. I therefore purposely set about marrying some of the cooking techniques and ingredients I had discovered abroad, to the Scottish recipes I knew. The result is in this book.

Preparation and cooking times

Preparation and cooking times are included at the head of the recipes as a general guide; preparation times, especially, are approximate and timings are usually rounded to the nearest 5 minutes.

Preparation times include the time taken to prepare ingredients in the list, but not to make any 'basic' recipe, such as a stock.

The cooking times given at the heads of the recipes denote cooking periods when the dish can be left largely unattended, e.g. baking, stewing, and not the total amount of cooking for the recipe. Always read and follow the timings given for the steps of the recipe in the method.

The descriptions often form a pocket travelogue of my time spent living abroad. Hot, sunny Provence is evident in my Aubergine Provençale, and Grilled Pepper and Olive Salad. The bold colours and flavours are reminiscent of the three months I spent as au pair in Arles with a French family: my first introduction to French country cooking at its best. I then spent one year in the Pyrenees and the exposure to a different style of cooking gave me recipes such as Semolina and Garlic Soup and Savoury Crêpe Layer. My next long-term stay abroad was in North Finland, where I enjoyed dishes such as Thick Pea Soup with Mustard, and Leeks with Mustard and Cheese. A three-year period spent in North Germany was my inspiration for recipes such as Hot Bread stuffed with Cream Cheese and Apple, Pork with Prunes, and Walnut and Pine Kernel Bread. Australia was the last country where I spent some time, and I was impressed by the locals' use of vegetables such as pumpkin and sweet potatoes; hence my recipes for Pumpkin Soup, and Sweet Potato with Orange and Brown Sugar Crust.

Many of the recipes – particularly for baking and soups – are modern variants from my Scottish upbringing. Carrot and Oatmeal Soup, Cloutie Dumpling and Border Tart are dishes I ate frequently as a child. Jams, jellies and chutneys were always home-made, so the inclusion of some preserves, such as Raspberry Jam with Drambuie and Microwave Lemon Curd, is of great significance to me. My particular love of both salads and pasta means that there are several recipes which introduce new taste combinations – I hope you enjoy the different uses of some traditional ingredients. Having never been a great fan of slices of fried black pudding for breakfast, but aware of its worth as a national dish of distinction, I have made it into a warm salad, with the crunchy addition of pistachio nuts. I have eaten many a delicious Salade Niçoise in France, and I decided to translate it into British terms by introducing a local fish; in this case I have used Arbroath smokie, but smoked mackerel is also good. Lasagne, which is usually served hot, is also delightful when served cold, with a tangy sauce of garlic and parsley and layered with tomatoes and good Scottish smoked salmon.

Some of the ingredients I like to use are fairly recent arrivals to this country, such as lemon grass (which I use in a stir-fried squid dish), or crème fraîche (which I use with smoked trout, chives and pasta). Many recipes use favourite local ingredients such as pheasant, salmon or lamb, with rather novel flavours. I have combined pheasant breasts with mango chutney and fresh mango, as the light game flavour of pheasant works beautifully with fruit of all sorts. Salmon is both inexpensive and widely available nowadays, so I do not think it sacrilegious to enliven and experiment with its accompanying sauces; hence my use of yellow peppers and basil, with this king of fish. I have also included lamb – not with the traditional mint or redcurrant jellies, but spread with a piquant black olive paste and surrounded by a crisp filo pastry coat. I am happy to admit that I have a very sweet tooth, so the preponderance of sticky-sounding recipes, such as Toffee Oat Squares, Ginger Millionaire's Shortbread or Caramel and Pecan Ice Cream are personal indulgences which I feel I must share in this compilation of my favourite recipes.

This book contains not only easy recipes and occasionally unconventional combinations of flavours, but, above all, my personal taste in both food and cooking, which has been greatly influenced by both travelling and living abroad. That is not to say that my roots have been forgotten, for I have mixed the old with the new. These recipes are not only my personal favourites, but ones that are made for sharing. I wish you happy and convivial eating.

SOUPS

THICK PEA SOUP WITH MUSTARD

Preparation time: 20 minutes + 8 hours soaking
+ 55 minutes cooking   Serves 4–5

375 g (12 oz) dried green split peas

15 g (½ oz) butter

300 g (10 oz) belly pork, or streaky pork rashers, sliced

1 onion, chopped

½ teaspoon salt

½ teaspoon dried marjoram

1 teaspoon Dijon mustard

900 ml (1½ pints) water

pepper

Dijon mustard, to serve

This pea soup is based on a Finnish recipe. It is hearty and thick – just the thing for the bitter cold I experienced while living just south of Lapland for a year. I was curious when I heard that on Thursdays, in winter, it was traditional to have pea soup and pancakes for lunch – I wondered about the main course. Having tasted this substantial soup followed by the sweet Yorkshire pudding-type pancakes, I held my peace.

Soak the peas in water overnight (or for at least 8 hours).

Drain them and rinse them well. Heat the butter in a large saucepan and add the pork. Brown on both sides, then add the onion and fry gently for 2–3 minutes. Add the peas, salt, pepper, marjoram, mustard and water. Bring to the boil; reduce to a simmer and cook, covered, for 45–50 minutes, until the peas are cooked.

With a slotted spoon, remove the pork and, when cool enough to handle, cut into chunks, discarding the fat. Purée the soup in a food processor or blender and season to taste. Return the meat to the soup. Reheat gently and serve, offering extra mustard in a small bowl.

SEMOLINA AND GARLIC SOUP

Preparation and cooking time: 15 minutes   Serves 3–4

900 ml (1½ pints) well-flavoured, light chicken stock

3 large garlic cloves, peeled

A French friend used to make this for me, while I was in the Pyrenées. Somehow soupe de semoule sounds more appetising than semolina soup, which is reminiscent of school semolina pudding. This soup, however, is not only quick to make, it is delicious and

1 large dried bay leaf (or 2
fresh leaves)

40 g (1½ oz) semolina

2 eggs, beaten

40 g (1½ oz) fresh
parmesan cheese, grated

salt and pepper

parmesan cheese, to serve

filling – just the thing to warm you up on a cold
winter day. The blending is best done with a balloon
whisk.

Bring the stock to the boil with the garlic, bay
leaf and plenty of salt and pepper. Boil for
about 2 minutes, then gradually whisk in the
semolina. Stir constantly for about 5–6
minutes, until the semolina is cooked. With a
slotted spoon, remove the bay leaf and garlic.
Remove the pan from the heat and, whisking
all the time, add the beaten eggs and cheese. Stir
well and serve at once in warmed bowls. Offer
extra parmesan cheese and plenty of crusty
bread.

MUSSEL SOUP

Preparation time: 30 minutes + 20 minutes cooking   Serves 4

1 tablespoon olive oil

25 g (1 oz) butter

1 leek, sliced thinly

1 fennel bulb, sliced finely

1 kg (2 lb) mussels,
scrubbed

125 ml (4 fl oz) dry white
wine

125 ml (4 fl oz) water

1 tablespoon Pernod

142 ml (¼ pint) carton of
double cream

2 tablespoons freshly
chopped parsley

salt and pepper

chopped parsley, to garnish

I have flavoured this hearty soup – more of a stew, in
fact – with fennel; and to enhance its aniseed flavour,
I have added Pernod. If you have no Pernod at home,
simply omit it; it is not worth buying a whole bottle
when a recipe calls for 1 tablespoon. Be sure to scrub
the mussels very well and remove the beards with
scissors. Throw away any mussels whose shells have
opened before cooking.

Heat the oil and butter in a large saucepan. Fry
the leek and fennel gently for about 10 minutes.
Add the mussels, wine, water and Pernod.
Increase the heat to high and cook for 4
minutes, covered, until all the mussel shells
have opened. Discard any which remain shut.
Transfer the mussels with a slotted spoon to a
warmed soup tureen.

Add the cream and parsley to the saucepan;
over a fairly high heat, cook for about 4–5
minutes, until the liquid has reduced slightly.
Season to taste, and then pour over the mussels.
Garnish with chopped parsley.

Serve at once, in large deep bowls, with
plenty of crusty bread.

CARROT AND OATMEAL SOUP

Preparation time: 25 minutes + 45 minutes cooking   Serves 4–5

25 g (1 oz) butter

2 leeks, white parts only, sliced thinly

500 g (1 lb) carrots, sliced thinly

1.2 litres (2 pints) chicken stock

½ teaspoon salt

zest of 1 orange

25 g (1 oz) medium or fine oatmeal

3 tablespoons milk

pepper

lovage leaves or flat parsley, finely chopped, to garnish

Oatmeal is often used in Scotland to thicken soups and stews. A fine or medium oatmeal should be used. I like to garnish this with some finely chopped lovage leaves, which have a flavour reminiscent of celery.

Melt the butter over a moderate heat, and add the leeks. Fry gently for 5 minutes. Add the carrots and fry gently for another 5 minutes.

Add the chicken stock, salt, pepper and orange zest. Bring to the boil, then simmer for 30 minutes over a low heat.

Meanwhile, soak the oatmeal in the milk for 15 minutes. Add the oatmeal mixture to the soup after the 30 minutes, and continue to cook, stirring regularly, for another 15 minutes. Season to taste. Purée or liquidise and serve piping hot, garnished with chopped lovage leaves or parsley.

COURGETTE, POTATO AND BRIE SOUP

Preparation time: 15 minutes + 25 minutes cooking   Serves 4

500 g (1 lb) courgettes, sliced

500 g (1 lb) potatoes, diced

1 tablespoon olive oil

900 ml (1½ pints) chicken stock

125 g (4 oz) soft ripe Brie, rind removed, chopped

salt and pepper

double cream, to serve

This soup is ideal if you have an unshapely piece of Brie left over from supper or dinner. It transforms a good vegetable soup into a smooth cheesy delight.

Over a very low heat, gently fry the courgettes and potatoes in the oil. Add salt and pepper to taste. Add the chicken stock and bring to the boil. Simmer until the potatoes are tender (about 15–20 minutes).

Liquidise the mixture in a food processor or blender, until smooth. Mix the Brie with a cupful of the liquid. Once it is well blended, pour back into the saucepan and reheat the soup, stirring constantly until the Brie has melted and the soup is sufficiently hot.

Season to taste and serve in warmed soup bowls, with a swirl of cream.

*Jerusalem Artichoke Soup
with Herb Croûtons*

*Courgette, Potato and
Brie Soup*

Red Pepper and Pear Soup

JERUSALEM ARTICHOKE SOUP WITH HERB CROÛTONS

Preparation time: 25 minutes + 30 minutes cooking
+ 10 minutes for the croûtons   Serves 4

For the croûtons:

2–3 tablespoons chopped fresh herbs

50 g (2 oz) unsalted butter, softened

1 tablespoon olive oil

2–3 slices of bread, crusts removed, cubed

For the soup:

500 g (1 !b) jerusalem artichokes

1 onion, chopped

600 ml (1 pint) chicken stock

300 ml (½ pint) milk

salt and pepper

cream, to serve

I adore the delicate, rather sweet flavour of jerusalem artichokes, particularly in a smooth soup or purée. The herb croûtons can be made with many different fresh herbs; I suggest thyme, sage, fennel, parsley, marjoram or coriander. They are good sprinkled over soups or salads, once they have been well drained on kitchen paper.

To make the herb croûtons, place the herbs and butter in a food processor and process until smooth (or beat together in a bowl by hand). Heat the herb butter and oil in a frying pan, and add the bread. Fry until golden brown and crispy, stirring often. Drain on kitchen paper.

To make the soup, peel the artichokes and chop them (you must do this quickly or they will turn brown; immersing them in water and lemon juice helps prevent discolouring). Place them in a saucepan with the onion and stock. Bring to the boil; reduce the heat to a simmer. Add the milk and cook for about 20 minutes, until the vegetables are tender.

Pour the contents into a food processor or blender and purée until smooth. Return the soup to a clean pan, reheat and season well. Serve piping hot, with a swirl of cream and some herb croûtons.

RED PEPPER AND PEAR SOUP

Preparation time: 20 minutes + 25 minutes cooking   Serves 4

2 tablespoons olive oil

1 onion, chopped

1 large carrot, chopped

500 g (1 lb) red peppers, de-seeded and chopped

750 ml (1¼ pints) chicken stock

1 large pear weighing about 250 g (8 oz), peeled and chopped

2 sprigs of fresh thyme

salt and pepper

To serve:

lightly whipped cream

Tabasco sauce

The tangy flavour of the red pepper and the sweetness of the pear combine beautifully in this colourful soup. To add extra 'heat' I like to shake in some Tabasco sauce at the end, over the cream.

Heat the oil in a large pan. Gently fry the onion, carrot and peppers, covered, until soft (for about 10 minutes). Add the stock and bring to the boil. Add the pear and thyme, and simmer, covered, for about 25 minutes until the vegetables are tender.

Remove the sprigs of thyme. Liquidise the soup in a blender or food processor in two batches, and add salt and pepper to taste. Sieve, to remove any pieces of pepper skin. Reheat, if necessary, and serve in warm soup bowls, with a little cream and a couple of dashes of Tabasco sauce.

CULLEN SKINK

Preparation time: 20 minutes + 30 minutes cooking   Serves 4–5

450 g (15 oz) smoked haddock fillets

300 ml (½ pint) water

2 onions, chopped finely

3 large potatoes weighing about 625 g (1¼ lb) in total, cut into chunks

450 ml (¾ pint) milk

25 g (1 oz) unsalted butter

salt and pepper

To serve:

double cream

chopped parsley

This recipe, which traditionally uses whole Finnan haddock, can also be made with undyed smoked haddock fillets. It is a perfect main-course supper dish, as its consistency is between that of a thick soup and a stew. Serve with crusty bread; or with thin oatcakes as a starter.

Place the haddock in the water in a large pan. Bring to the boil, then simmer for 8–10 minutes until the fish is just cooked.

Remove the fish with a slotted spoon. Skin and flake the fish, then set aside. Add the onions and potatoes to the pan, with plenty of pepper. Cover and cook over a moderate heat for about 12–15 minutes until the vegetables are tender.

Remove the pan from the heat and mash the contents roughly, with a fork or masher. Add the milk and the butter. Bring to the boil and simmer for a couple of minutes; then add the flaked fish and reheat gently for another couple of minutes. Season to taste (the addition of salt depends on the saltiness of the fish).

Serve piping hot in warmed soup bowls, with a swirl of cream and sprinkled with lots of freshly chopped parsley.

PUMPKIN SOUP

Preparation time: 30 minutes + 55 minutes cooking   Serves 4–6

25 g (1 oz) unsalted butter

1 onion, chopped

½ teaspoon ground cumin

½ teaspoon ground coriander

1 kg (2 lb) pumpkin (peeled weight – you will need a small pumpkin for this, about 1.25–1.75 kg/ 3–4 lb), cubed

1.2 litres (2 pints) chicken stock

salt and pepper

To serve:

whipped cream

chopped fresh chives or chervil

During the few months I lived in Sydney, it never ceased to amaze me how many ways pumpkin was used in recipes – not only in pies and soups, but grated into breads or scones, as fillings for ravioli, or roasted in chunks around the Sunday joint. This soup is very simple, once you have peeled the thick skin off. Do not waste the seeds: they make wonderful snacks to accompany drinks. Simply wash the seeds and, with the water still clinging to them, place them in a roasting tin with a knob of butter. Roast at the top of the oven (Gas Mark 5/190°C/ 375°F) for about 25–30 minutes. Remove, sprinkle with some salt and drain on kitchen paper.

Melt the butter in a large pan, add the onion and fry gently for about 5 minutes. Add the cumin and coriander and fry for another 2–3 minutes. Add the pumpkin to the pan. Stir to coat the pumpkin with the butter. Add the stock and ½ a teaspoon of salt, bring to the boil and simmer, covered, for about 45 minutes.

Purée or liquidise in a food processor or blender. Reheat and season to taste. To serve, ladle into warmed bowls and top with a little cream and freshly snipped chives or chervil.

Cullen Skink
Pumpkin Soup

EGGS AND CHEESE

EGGS BAKED WITH SPINACH AND SMOKED HADDOCK

Preparation time: 10 minutes + 15–20 minutes poaching
+ 15–20 minutes cooking   Serves 4

*250 g (8 oz) Arbroath
smokie, or undyed smoked
haddock fillet*

300 ml (½ pint) milk

*250 g (8 oz) fresh spinach,
stalks removed*

*1 tablespoon melted butter
plus 25 g (1 oz) butter*

25 g (1 oz) plain flour

juice of ½ lemon

4 eggs

*25 g (1 oz) fresh parmesan
cheese, grated*

salt, pepper and nutmeg

*I am a great fan of Arbroath smokies – not only
because my sister, who lives in Arbroath, often
brings me freshly smoked, succulent smokies, but also
because of their versatility. Here they flavour a white
sauce (it is important to leave the skins on when they
are flavouring the milk as they add to the smoky
taste) and top a combination of spinach and eggs,
rather like Eggs Florentine. Undyed smoked haddock
fillet is a suitable substitute.*

Preheat the oven to Gas Mark 2/150°C/300°F.

Place the smokie in an ovenproof dish with
the milk and heat in the oven, to loosen the skin
and flavour the milk – this should take about 20
minutes. (If using smoked haddock, poach in
the milk until just cooked – about 15 minutes.)

Place the spinach, with the water clinging to
its leaves, in a pan with the melted butter and
cook for 2–3 minutes, until just beginning to
'wilt'. Drain well and chop roughly. Season
with salt, pepper and nutmeg to taste. Divide
the spinach between 4 well-buttered 8 cm
(3-inch) ramekin dishes, moulding it into 'nest'
shapes. Increase the oven temperature to Gas
Mark 5/190°C/375°F.

Remove the fish from the milk, discard any
skin and bones and strain the milk. Flake the
fish. Melt the remaining butter in a pan, stir in
the flour and cook for 1 minute, then add the
flavoured milk, bring to the boil and simmer
for about 5 minutes, until thick. Season with
pepper and lemon juice to taste, then gently
fold in the flaked fish.

Carefully break an egg into each spinach
'nest' and season. Spoon the fish sauce over the
top, taking care not to break the yolk. Gently

smooth the top and sprinkle with some parmesan cheese. Bake on the top shelf of the preheated oven for about 12–14 minutes.

Serve at once, with some fresh, warm bread.

SAVOURY CRÊPE LAYER

Preparation time: 55 minutes + 30 minutes standing
+ 20 minutes baking   Serves 4–5

For the crêpes:

125 g (4 oz) plain flour, sifted

a pinch of salt

1 egg

300 ml (½ pint) milk

butter for frying

For the sauce:

50 g (2 oz) butter

50 g (2 oz) flour

450 ml (¾ pint) milk

For the filling:

1 teaspoon oil for frying

450 g (15 oz) lean minced lamb

4 tablespoons tomato purée

2 teaspoons freshly chopped rosemary

125 g (4 oz) iceberg lettuce, shredded finely

1 tablespoon milk

50 g (2 oz) Cheddar cheese, grated

salt and pepper

The quantities given for the crêpes make about 10 × 18 cm (7-inch) thin crêpes, although you only need 5 in this recipe so freeze the rest for another time. Most crêpes or pancakes are rolled or folded around fillings, but here they are layered with the filling to form a high cake which has a combination of delicious flavours – lamb, cheese and crunchy iceberg lettuce. Once it is baked, it looks rather stunning. Serve it with a green salad tossed in an olive oil and lemon dressing.

To make the crêpes, blend all the ingredients in a food processor, then leave for about 30 minutes. Lightly butter a non-stick frying-pan and fry 5 crêpes, turning them when bubbles appear.

To make the sauce, melt the butter in a pan. Stir in the flour and cook for 1 minute, then gradually whisk in the milk. Bring to the boil and simmer until thick (about 5 minutes).

Heat the oil in a pan and fry the minced lamb gently until browned. Add 2 tablespoons of the tomato purée and the rosemary and cook for about 15 minutes, over a low heat. Season with salt and pepper.

Remove 2 tablespoons of the white sauce and set aside. Mix the iceberg lettuce with the remaining sauce and season well. Preheat the oven to Gas Mark 6/200°C/400°F.

In a buttered, shallow oven-proof dish (about 23 cm/9 inches in diameter), place 1 crêpe. Spread it with ½ tablespoon of the tomato purée, then with half of the iceberg lettuce

(continued on page 22)

19

Eggs baked with Spinach
and Smoked Haddock

Thyme and
Goat's Cheese Tart

Savoury Crêpe Layer

mixture. Place another crêpe on top, spread with ½ tablespoon of the tomato purée, then with half of the lamb mixture. Repeat with the remaining sauce and lamb and 2 more crêpes.

Add the milk to the remaining white sauce in order to thin it. Place the last crêpe on top of the pile of crêpes, pour over the thinned-down sauce, sprinkle the cheese on top and bake in the oven for about 20 minutes, until golden brown on top.

Serve at once, cut into wedges.

THYME AND GOAT'S CHEESE TART

Preparation time: 25 minutes + 2½–3 hours chilling
+ 15 minutes baking 'blind' + 30–35 minutes cooking
+ 20 minutes cooling   Serves 8

For the pastry:

275 g (9 oz) plain flour, sifted

¾ teaspoon salt

150 g (5 oz) unsalted butter

1 egg, beaten

1 tablespoon olive oil

For the filling:

250 g (8 oz) goat's cheese, rind removed, chopped roughly

200 ml (7 fl oz) carton of crème fraîche

5 eggs, beaten

3–4 teaspoons fresh thyme leaves

50 g (2 oz) pine kernels

1 tablespoon olive oil

pepper

The flavours in this tart are superb. The crisp pastry has a lining of golden pine kernels, which is topped with a combination of fresh thyme, goat's cheese and crème fraîche. It is best eaten warm, either as a starter or with a fresh green salad for lunch.

To make the pastry, place the flour, salt and butter in a food processor. Mix briefly, then add the egg mixed with the oil through the feeder tube, until the mixture forms a ball. (To make the pastry by hand, place the flour and salt in a bowl. Cut the butter into cubes and rub it into the flour, until the mixture resembles breadcrumbs. Mix the egg and olive oil together then add them to the flour mixture and combine gently with a knife. Collect the mixture together with one hand and knead very briefly to a smooth dough.) Wrap in clingfilm and chill in the refrigerator for 1 hour.

Roll out the pastry and line a lightly buttered, shallow 28 cm (11-inch) flan tin with it. Prick the base and chill for 1½–2 hours.

Preheat the oven to Gas Mark 6/200°C/ 400°F. Bake the pastry 'blind', with baking parchment and baking beans, for 10 minutes; remove the beans and parchment and cook for another 5 minutes. Remove and cool. Reduce the oven temperature to Gas Mark 4/180°C/350°F.

To make the filling, place the goat's cheese, crème fraîche, eggs and pepper in a food processor. Add the thyme leaves and process until well blended. Fry the pine kernels for about 2–3 minutes in the oil until golden brown, then cool slightly.

Sprinkle the pine kernels on the base of the tart, and top with the goat's cheese mixture. Bake near the top of the oven for about 30–35 minutes, until the filling is puffed and golden brown.

Allow to cool for about 20 minutes before serving warm.

HERBY SCOTCH EGGS

Preparation time: 30 minutes + 20 minutes chilling
+ 16 minutes cooking   Makes 5

6 slices of bread, crusts removed, processed into crumbs

500 g (1 lb) pork sausage meat

2 tablespoons porridge oats

3 tablespoons freshly chopped mixed herbs

5 eggs, hard-boiled

2 teaspoons flour, seasoned

1 egg, beaten

oil, to deep-fry

These scotch eggs are full of flavour and colour. The sausage meat is flavoured with freshly chopped herbs – I like a mixture of parsley, marjoram and thyme, but sage, basil or chives all work very well. The outer crust should be made with freshly toasted breadcrumbs. They are ideal for picnic or lunch-box food.

Toast the breadcrumbs under the grill for about 5 minutes, turning regularly, until golden.

Combine the sausage meat with the oats and herbs, and divide into five. Shell the eggs and roll them in the flour. Mould the sausage meat around each egg, making sure they are evenly covered. Coat the eggs with the beaten egg and the crumbs. Place on a plate in the refrigerator for 20 minutes.

Heat the oil and deep-fry the eggs in batches – 8 minutes for each batch. Remove and drain well on kitchen paper.

Serve slightly warm or at room temperature, cut into halves or quarters.

HOT BREAD STUFFED WITH CREAM CHEESE AND APPLE

Preparation time: 25 minutes + 20 minutes cooling
+ 60 minutes cooking   Serves 8

1 french loaf

3 teaspoons olive oil

½ onion, chopped finely

400 g (13 oz) minced pork

1 teaspoon paprika

1 tablespoon tomato purée

250 g (8 oz) full fat cream cheese with garlic and parsley

1 large Granny Smith apple, grated

125 g (4 oz) Cheddar cheese, grated

salt and pepper

When I lived in Germany, I was impressed by the number of dishes, both hot and cold, that were made with their many breads – rye, 'dreikorn', 'vollkorn' and farmhouse loaves – to name but four. This is my version of a favourite hot stuffed bread we ate there: a french loaf (it should weigh about 400 g/13 oz and be wide rather than long) stuffed with cheese, pork and apple. It can be prepared in advance and refrigerated for up to 4 hours.

Cut the bread in half horizontally (I find it easier to leave the two sides slightly 'hinged' together). With your fingers, remove as much of the soft bread as possible to create sufficient space for the filling. Preheat the oven to Gas Mark 6/200°C/400°F.

Heat 1 teaspoon of the oil in a pan and fry the onion gently for 1 minute. Add the meat and cook until brown all over. Add the paprika, tomato purée, salt and pepper, and cook for a further 25 minutes, uncovered. Allow to cool for about 20 minutes.

Soften the cream cheese slightly, then spread it inside both halves of the loaf. Spoon the meat into one of the halves, packing it down well. Put the grated apple over the top, and sprinkle with the Cheddar cheese. Drizzle the remaining olive oil over the filling, then 'close' the loaf, pressing the other side down carefully. Wrap very tightly in lightly oiled foil and bake in the oven for 20–30 minutes, or until the cheese has melted and everything is piping hot.

It is easier to serve this by cutting it into slices with an electric knife or an extremely sharp bread knife.

Picnic Loaf with Mozzarella and Feta Cheese
Hot Bread stuffed with Cream Cheese and Apple

PICNIC LOAF WITH MOZZARELLA AND FETA CHEESE

Preparation time: 20 minutes + overnight
'weighting down'   Serves 8–10

1 ciabatta loaf

4 tablespoons extra-virgin olive oil

1–2 tablespoons black olive paste

3 tablespoons pesto sauce

175 g (6 oz) mozzarella cheese, sliced

125 g (4 oz) feta cheese, sliced

15 g (½ oz) packet of rocket, stalks removed

1 extra large tomato, sliced

6–8 large basil leaves

6–8 sun-dried tomatoes in oil, drained and halved

salt and pepper

This is wonderful for any picnic – even the most wind-blown, chilly British picnic – as the flavours are so full of the Mediterranean, you can almost imagine that you are in hotter climes. Mine is vegetarian, but you can also layer in some slices of salami or add some artichoke hearts, pine kernels, black olives or tuna. Baby spinach leaves could be used as an alternative to rocket. It is essential to make it the day before, for all the flavours to combine and to weight it down, so that the natural juices of the ingredients are absorbed.

Slice the loaf horizontally and remove some of the soft bread, to make room for the filling. Brush the inside of both halves with 3 tablespoons of the olive oil. Spread one half with the olive paste and the other with the pesto. Layer the slices of mozzarella and feta cheeses, rocket, tomato, basil and sun–dried tomatoes in the bottom half of the loaf. Season lightly as you layer. Finish with another spoonful of the olive oil, and then carefully place the other half of the loaf on top. Wrap tightly in double foil, then place in the refrigerator overnight, well weighted down.

To serve, unwrap the loaf and cut it into thick slices. Eat at room temperature, not straight from the refrigerator.

CHEDDAR AND APPLE SOUFFLÉ

Preparation time: 30 minutes + 35–40 minutes cooking   Serves 4

50 g (2 oz) butter

40 g (1½ oz) plain flour

300 ml (½ pint) milk

½ teaspoon Dijon mustard

75 g (3 oz) mature Cheddar, grated

4 eggs, separated

2 dessert apples (preferably Cox's Orange Pippin or Granny Smith), peeled and diced

salt and pepper

This is a fairly classic cheese soufflé with a surprise element at the base of the dish: some finely chopped apples, which add both sweetness and crunch. I prefer to use a mature Cheddar, such as Isle of Mull Cheddar, but any strongly flavoured farmhouse Cheddar will do. To ring the changes, you can also use pecorino or parmesan in the soufflé, and chopped pears instead of apples. I like to serve this with a salad of celery, walnuts and unpeeled apples in yogurt and lemon juice.

Preheat the oven to Gas Mark 5/190°C/375°F. Melt the butter in a saucepan, stir in the flour and cook for 1 minute. Remove from the heat and gradually blend in the milk. Return to the heat and cook until thickened, whisking all the time. Beat in the mustard, salt, pepper and cheese. Cool for a couple of minutes, then add the egg yolks. Whisk the egg whites until stiff, but not dry. Using a metal spoon, fold a quarter of the egg whites into the cheese mixture, then gently fold in the rest.

Butter a 1.5 litre (2½ pint) soufflé dish. Place the apples at the base of the dish, then pour in the soufflé mixture. (It should come to just below the rim of the dish.) Bake in the oven for 35–40 minutes, or until well risen and golden brown. (You can also bake in individual 8 cm (3-inch) soufflé dishes, for about 15 minutes.) Serve at once.

PARMESAN AND HERB SCONES

Preparation time: 15 minutes + 10 minutes baking   Makes 8–10

175 g (6 oz) self-raising
flour

1 teaspoon baking powder

a pinch of salt

50 g (2 oz) Granary®
flour

50 g (2 oz) unsalted butter

2–3 teaspoons fresh thyme
leaves

1 tablespoon grated fresh
parmesan cheese

2–3 tablespoons milk

1 egg, beaten

milk, to glaze

These scones are absolutely delicious, and so quick to make. You can substitute chopped fresh rosemary or marjoram for the thyme, and mature Cheddar for the parmesan.

Preheat the oven to Gas Mark 7/220°C/425°F. Sift the self-raising flour with the baking powder and salt into a bowl, then add the Granary® flour. Rub the butter into the flours and stir in the thyme and parmesan. Add the milk and egg, to make a soft dough, then roll out to 1 cm (½-inch) thickness and cut into rounds with a 6 cm (2½-inch) scone/pastry cutter. Brush the tops with a little milk. Place on a buttered baking sheet and bake near the top of the oven for about 10 minutes. Cool slightly on a wire rack, then serve warm, with unsalted butter.

POTATO AND CHEESE SCONES

Preparation time: 15–20 minutes + 12 minutes cooking   Makes 8–10

1 large potato weighing
about 250 g (8 oz), boiled

50 g (2 oz) melted butter

40–50 g (1½–2 oz) plain
flour, sifted

25 g (1 oz) mature
Cheddar cheese, grated

salt and pepper

Tattie scones (potato scones) are traditional Scottish fare, and can be eaten toasted, fried with bacon, or plain and served with butter. It is best to use a floury potato, such as King Edward or Pentland Squire. They are not cooked in the oven, but on an iron girdle (the Scots' word for griddle). A heavy-based frying-pan is a good substitute. Usually eaten at high tea, they are also ideal – instead of bread – for accompanying a hearty soup.

Mash the potato with half of the butter while still warm. Then add enough flour to combine well, without becoming too dry. Add the cheese and season well. On a floured surface, roll the mixture out to about 5 mm (¼-inch) thickness and cut into 2 circles, and then cut the circles into quarters. Prick with a fork and sprinkle a little flour over the surface.

Heat the remaining butter in a large frying-pan (or, ideally, a hot girdle) and cook for about 3 minutes on each side until browned and firm. (This should be done in 2 batches.) Drain on kitchen paper.

Serve warm, with or without butter.

GRILLED GOAT'S CHEESE WITH TARRAGON

Preparation time: 10 minutes + 10 minutes baking   Serves 4

½ french stick or 4 thick slices of wholemeal bread

4 slices of goat's cheese (about 2 cm/¾ inch thick) or individual cheeses

4 tablespoons extra-virgin olive oil

1 tablespoon tarragon vinegar, or white wine vinegar

1 tablespoon chopped fresh tarragon

mixed salad leaves, such as lamb's lettuce, frisée, cos lettuce, baby spinach

salt and pepper

fresh tarragon sprigs, to garnish

A 'log' shape of goat's cheese is ideal for this because you can cut slices to fit the bread. Even better, however, are individual goat's cheeses which have been marinated in olive oil and herbs, as they will not dry out once baked. It is easy to marinate at home, by simply covering individual cheeses (in a large jar) with extra-virgin olive oil and some sprigs of fresh herbs – in this case, tarragon, although basil, rosemary and thyme are also good. With a tight-fitting lid, they should keep in the fridge for a couple of months.

Preheat the oven to Gas Mark 5/190°C/375°F. Slice the french stick into rounds (or cut the wholemeal bread, using a pastry cutter), about the same thickness as the cheese. Place a round of cheese on each, and place on an oiled baking sheet. Drizzle 1 tablespoon of the oil over the tops. Bake at the top of the oven for about 10 minutes until the cheese has melted.

In a screw-top jar, shake together the remaining oil, vinegar, tarragon, salt and pepper. Toss the salad leaves in the dressing, then arrange on individual plates. Place the baked cheese, straight from the oven, on to the plate. Garnish with fresh tarragon and serve at once.

SALADS AND VEGETABLES

ROAST BEEF SALAD WITH ROCKET MAYONNAISE

Preparation time: 15 minutes + 20 minutes cooking   Serves 4–5

500 g (1 lb) beef fillet

pepper

hazelnut oil, for brushing

a handful of rocket leaves, to serve

For the mayonnaise:

25 g (1 oz) rocket, trimmed

4 tablespoons mayonnaise

2 tablespoons greek-style yogurt

½ teaspoon horseradish sauce

salt and pepper

Rocket is a favourite herb and apart from mixing it with salad leaves, I like to serve it in a mayonnaise with cold beef. Watercress could be used as an alternative to rocket, if required. The mayonnaise is also excellent served with cold poached salmon.

Preheat the oven to Gas Mark 6/200°C/400°F. Tie the beef with string, to keep its shape, then season with plenty of pepper. Brush lightly with hazelnut oil, then place in a roasting tin and roast in the preheated oven for 20 minutes (for rare beef). Remove and cool completely.

Place all the mayonnaise ingredients in a food processor or blender and process until well blended. Season to taste.

Once the beef is cold, cut it into very thin slices and arrange them, with some rocket leaves, on a serving plate. Either spoon the mayonnaise over the top or serve it separately in a bowl.

ARBROATH SMOKIE SALADE NIÇOISE

Preparation time: 40 minutes   Serves 4

2 Arbroath smokies or smoked mackerel fillets

crisp salad leaves, such as iceberg, cos or little gem

4–6 unpeeled, waxy potatoes, cooked and quartered

Instead of tuna (canned or fresh) in a salade niçoise, I have introduced British smoked fish – my favourite being Arbroath smokies, but smoked mackerel is also very good. The fish should be 'hot-smoked', which requires no further cooking. The basic components of the salad are eggs, anchovy, olives, lettuce, tomatoes and tuna. I remember eating it with cooked waxy potatoes in the south of France, and this addition makes it a substantial main meal.

4–6 large tomatoes, quartered	Remove and discard the skin and any bones from the smoked fish, and flake the flesh into chunks. Shake all the dressing ingredients together in a screw-top jar. Place the lettuce leaves, potatoes, tomatoes and beans in a large salad bowl and toss in most of the dressing, to coat. Arrange the eggs and fish on top, then finish with the olives and anchovies spiralled out like a pizza topping. Pour over the remaining dressing and garnish with the basil or parsley. Serve with plenty of warm crusty bread.
125 g (4 oz) green beans, blanched for 1 minute	
4 eggs, hard-boiled and quartered	
12 black olives, drained	
50 g (2 oz) can of anchovy fillets, drained	
freshly chopped basil or parsley, to garnish	
For the dressing:	*(Also pictured on the front cover)*
6 tablespoons extra-virgin olive oil	
2 tablespoons wine vinegar	
1 garlic clove, crushed	
½ teaspoon Dijon mustard	
salt and pepper	

BLACK PUDDING AND PISTACHIO SALAD

Preparation time: 25 minutes   Serves 4

1 bag of mixed salad leaves	*This rather unlikely combination produces a warm salad which is full of flavour and has a good crunchy texture. I like to use a bag of ready-prepared salad leaves that includes feuille de chêne. As an alternative, baby spinach, lamb's lettuce or round lettuce are also good.*
3 tablespoons olive oil	
2 slices of bread, crusts removed, cubed	
1 tablespoon walnut oil	
175 g (6 oz) black pudding, skin removed, cut into bite-size chunks	Place the salad leaves in a large salad bowl and season with salt and pepper. Heat 2 tablespoons of the olive oil in a frying pan, and fry the bread cubes for 2–3 minutes, turning them as they cook. Remove and drain on kitchen paper.
50 g (2 oz) shelled pistachios	
1 tablespoon red wine vinegar or balsamic vinegar	Add the remaining olive oil and the walnut oil to the frying pan. Heat until hot, then add the chunks of black pudding and fry for about 2–3 minutes, turning them as they cook, until crunchy outside and just cooked through. Add
salt and pepper	

(continued on page 34)

31

Roast Beef Salad with Rocket Mayonnaise

Arbroath Smokie Salade Niçoise

*Black Pudding and
Pistachio Salad*

the pistachios and fry, stirring all the time, for about 30 seconds. Add the vinegar and stir well, then remove from the heat and pour the hot mixture over the salad leaves. Add the bread croûtons, toss everything together and serve on 4 individual plates.

COUSCOUS AND MINT SALAD

Preparation time: 20 minutes + 20 minutes 'standing'   Serves 4–6

200 g (7 oz) couscous

300 ml (½ pint) boiling water

½ teaspoon salt

8 tablespoons chopped fresh mint

4 tablespoons chopped fresh parsley, preferably flat leaf

3–4 tomatoes, skinned and chopped

½ cucumber, chopped finely

lettuce leaves, to serve

For the dressing:

4 tablespoons olive oil

1 tablespoon lemon juice or white wine vinegar

1 garlic clove, crushed

salt and pepper

Nowadays most couscous available in shops is pre-cooked, so it needs only a very short steaming time. In this recipe, olive oil and lemon juice are mixed into the couscous, with lots of mint and parsley, to give a refreshing, colourful salad. It is a delicious accompaniment to barbecue food.

Place the couscous in a bowl. Pour over enough boiling water to just cover the couscous. Fork the mixture through, then cover with a double tea towel and leave to stand.

To make the dressing, shake all the ingredients together in a screw-top jar.

After 15–20 minutes fork through the couscous again to remove any lumps; add the salt and dressing. Mix the mint and parsley into the couscous with the tomatoes and cucumber. Serve in a large bowl lined with lettuce.

ROSEMARY ROAST POTATOES

Preparation time: 20 minutes + 55 minutes cooking   Serves 4

750 g (1½ lb) large potatoes, such as Maris Piper or Cara

These are roast potatoes with a difference. They are redolent of garlic and rosemary: ideal, therefore, to accompany roast lamb or indeed any roast meat or game. Once you have removed the potatoes from the

3 tablespoons olive oil

1–2 heaped tablespoons finely chopped fresh rosemary

2 large garlic cloves

salt and pepper

oil, you can use the garlic and rosemary-flavoured oil to fry eggs or vegetables such as courgettes, aubergines or peppers.

Preheat the oven to Gas Mark 5/190°C/375°F. Cut the potatoes into large chunks, then parboil them for no more than 5 minutes. Drain well, cover with a clean tea towel and leave to dry for about 10 minutes.

Place the potatoes in an ovenproof dish and drizzle over the oil. Sprinkle with salt, pepper and the rosemary leaves. Add the garlic cloves. Place near the top of the oven and, basting every 15 minutes, cook for 45–50 minutes, until golden brown and crisp.

Remove the potatoes with a slotted spoon, drain on kitchen paper and serve at once.

LEEKS WITH MUSTARD AND CHEESE

Preparation time: 15 minutes + 12 minutes cooking   Serves 4–6

625 g (1¼ lb) small leeks

50 g (2 oz) unsalted butter

2 tablespoons coarse-grain mustard

50 g (2 oz) Cheddar cheese, grated

Leeks are among my favourite vegetables and I think steaming is one of the kindest ways to treat them. A mixture of coarse-grain mustard and cheese provides a delicious topping, once it has been browned under the grill.

Preheat the grill to hot. Keep the leeks whole, if small, or cut diagonally into thick slices. Steam for 6–8 minutes, depending on size; test with a knife to check whether they are cooked – they should still be slightly crisp. Meanwhile, warm the butter until it is soft, then add the mustard; stir in the cheese and combine well.

When cooked, drain the leeks well and place in a flameproof shallow dish. Dot with the mustard butter. Place under the grill for about 3–5 minutes, until bubbly and golden brown. Serve at once.

THREE TOMATO SALAD WITH BASIL VINAIGRETTE

Preparation time: 15 minutes
Serves 4–5

2 extra large tomatoes

a pinch of caster sugar

3–4 plum tomatoes, sliced thinly

1 × 250 g (8 oz) punnet of cherry tomatoes, halved

salt and pepper

basil leaves, to garnish

For the vinaigrette:

4 tablespoons extra-virgin olive oil

1 tablespoon balsamic vinegar or sherry vinegar

2 teaspoons pesto sauce

salt and pepper

In this recipe, the simplicity of a fresh tomato salad is enhanced by a basil-flavoured dressing. I suggest using 3 different types of tomatoes, but if you find others, such as yellow tomatoes, then add them too. This salad should be served with plenty of crusty bread to mop up the juices.

Cut the extra large tomatoes into fairly thick slices and place on individual serving plates. Seasoning with salt, pepper and a pinch of sugar as you work, top with thinner slices of the plum tomatoes, then with the halved cherry tomatoes.

To make the vinaigrette, place all the ingredients in a screw-top jar and shake vigorously. Season to taste, then pour a little over each tomato salad. Garnish with some fresh basil leaves.

GRILLED PEPPER AND OLIVE SALAD

Preparation time: 15 minutes + 10 minutes grilling + 30 minutes 'steaming'
Serves 6

2 large red peppers, de-seeded and halved

1 large green pepper, de-seeded and halved

1 large yellow pepper, de-seeded and halved

4 tablespoons extra-virgin olive oil

1 tablespoon sherry vinegar

1 garlic clove, crushed

salt and pepper

black olives, to serve

If you prefer, the peppers can be roasted, rather than grilled, in a hot oven (Gas Mark 6/200°C/400°F) for 25–30 minutes. A variety of different-coloured peppers makes the dish look bright and summery. You should offer plenty of fresh crusty bread with this to mop up all the delicious juices.

Preheat the grill to very hot. Place the peppers on a large sheet of foil in the grill pan and drizzle with 1 tablespoon of the oil. Grill for 5–10 minutes, until charred and blistered.

*Three Tomato Salad with Basil Vinaigrette
Grilled Pepper and Olive Salad*

Remove from the grill, wrap up tightly in the foil and leave for about 30 minutes. The steam will loosen the pepper skins.

Once they are cool enough to handle, remove the skins and cut into slivers. Place (or arrange, like the spokes of a wheel) in a large shallow bowl. Mix together the remaining oil with the vinegar, garlic, salt and pepper, and pour over the peppers. Either toss or leave 'arranged' and garnish with plenty of black olives.

VEGETABLE STRUDEL

Preparation time: 45–55 minutes + 20 minutes cooling + 30 minutes baking   Makes 4 strudels – serves 6–8

1 tablespoon olive oil

25 g (1 oz) butter

1 onion, chopped

2 garlic cloves, chopped

3 teaspoons ground cumin

500 g (1 lb) Savoy cabbage, shredded finely

250 g (8 oz) mushrooms, sliced

50 g (2 oz) sultanas

1 Granny Smith apple, peeled and grated

salt and pepper

soured cream, to serve

For the pastry:

16 sheets of fresh filo pastry

100 g (3½ oz) unsalted butter, melted

This is wonderful party food – a vegetarian main course, an unusual starter or a moveable picnic dish. Be sure to keep the sheets of filo pastry covered with a slightly damp tea towel while you work, otherwise they will become dry, brittle and unusable.

Preheat the oven to Gas Mark 6/200°C/400°F. Heat the oil and butter in a very large pan and gently fry the onion and garlic until transparent. Add the cumin, stir for half a minute, then add the cabbage and mushrooms. Stir well and cook for 3–4 minutes, stirring often, or until the cabbage is just cooked but still crisp. Remove from the heat; add the sultanas, apple and seasoning to taste. Place in a fine sieve over a bowl, to drain off any excess liquid and leave to cool.

Spread one sheet of filo on to a work surface and brush with some melted butter. Place a second sheet on top, brush with butter, then continue with two more sheets, finishing by brushing the fourth sheet with melted butter. Place a quarter of the vegetable mixture on to one end of the sheet, about 2 cm (¾ inch) from the sides (Fig. 1). Fold in the sides and end, and roll up carefully, like a swiss roll (Fig. 2). Remove very carefully to a greased baking

38

sheet, with join underneath, and brush with melted butter.

Make the other strudels in exactly the same way, and prick the tops with a sharp knife a couple of times. Bake for 25–30 minutes until crisp and golden. Serve hot or at room temperature, with a bowl of soured cream.

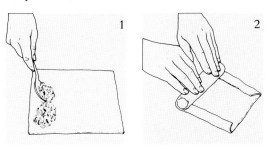

SWEET POTATO WITH ORANGE AND BROWN SUGAR CRUST

Preparation time: 15 minutes + 45–55 minutes cooking   Serves 4–5

1 kg (2 lb) sweet potatoes, chopped

50 g (2 oz) butter

zest and juice of 1 orange

1 heaped tablespoon soft brown sugar

a pinch of cinnamon

salt and pepper

Sweet potatoes are delicious when baked or boiled and mashed with butter. They have an orange flesh, which loses none of its intense colour when cooked. The natural sweetness of the vegetable is enhanced by the addition of brown sugar and cinnamon.

Preheat the oven to Gas Mark 2/150°C/300°F. Boil the sweet potatoes in lightly salted boiling water for 10–15 minutes. Drain well, then mash with 40 g (1½ oz) of the butter. Season with salt and pepper, then add the orange zest and juice.

Turn the mixture into a casserole dish, sprinkle with the brown sugar and cinnamon, and dot the remaining butter over the top.

Bake on the top shelf of the oven for 30–40 minutes, until warmed through and the sugar has melted.

Sweet Potato with Orange
and Brown Sugar Crust

Courgettes with Lemon
and Parmesan

Vegetable Strudel

COURGETTES WITH LEMON AND PARMESAN

Preparation time: 15 minutes + 25 minutes cooking   Serves 5–6

25 g (1 oz) butter

500 g (1 lb) baby courgettes, cut diagonally into slices about 15 mm (⅝ inch) thick

juice of ½ lemon

40 g (1½ oz) fresh parmesan cheese, grated

4 tablespoons double cream

zest of 1 lemon

salt and pepper

For this recipe, try to obtain baby courgettes. If you have both time and patience, arrange the courgettes in regular lines in the dish, once you have fried them. Otherwise, just tip them in – they taste just as good.

Preheat the oven to Gas Mark 5/190°C/375°F. Melt the butter in a large frying-pan and gently fry the courgettes for about 5 minutes, until just beginning to colour. Transfer to an ovenproof dish. Sprinkle them with salt, pepper and the lemon juice. Top with the parmesan cheese. Cover the dish with foil and bake in the oven for about 20 minutes.

Heat the cream gently with the lemon zest in a small saucepan, until very hot but not boiling. Remove the dish from the oven and immediately pour the cream over the courgettes. Serve at once.

DOUBLE TOMATO TARTS

Preparation time: 30 minutes + 1 hour chilling + 10 minutes 'blind' baking + 1 hour 'draining' + 1 hour 'softening' + 30 minutes baking + 15 minutes cooling   Makes 6

For the pastry:

250 g (8 oz) plain flour, sifted

¼ teaspoon salt

100 g (3½ oz) unsalted butter, chopped

1 egg yolk

1 tablespoon oil (preferably from the jar of sun-dried tomatoes)

For the filling:

3 extra large tomatoes

The 'double' in the tarts is fresh tomatoes and sun-dried tomatoes. It is important to cut and drain the fresh tomatoes before using them, so that their moisture does not leak into the pastry. The filling is rather rich, so I serve these with a little tossed salad as a starter before a light main course.

To make the pastry, place the flour, salt and butter in a food processor and process until it resembles breadcrumbs (or place in a bowl and rub in by hand). Add the egg yolk and oil and mix until the dough forms a soft, not sticky, ball (adding a tablespoon of water if necessary). Chill in the refrigerator for at least 30 minutes, then roll out to fit 6 × 10 cm (4-inch) tart tins,

250 g (8 oz) mascarpone cheese

150 g (5 oz) Gruyère cheese, grated

2 teaspoons dried oregano, or 2 tablespoons fresh oregano leaves

9 sun-dried tomatoes in seasoned oil, well drained and halved

salt and pepper

preferably loose-bottomed. Prick with a fork and chill for at least 30 minutes.

Halve the fresh tomatoes, sprinkle them with salt and place them, cut-side down, on a rack, over kitchen paper. Leave them to 'drain' for an hour.

Preheat the oven to Gas Mark 6/200°C/ 400°F. To make the filling, place the mascarpone, Gruyère, salt, pepper and oregano in a food processor and process until well blended (or beat together in a bowl). Leave at room temperature to soften for an hour.

Bake the pastry shells 'blind' for 10 minutes, then remove and cool. Reduce the oven to Gas Mark 5/190°C/375°F. Spoon the filling evenly between the 6 tins. (Do not worry if it is not very even.) Wipe the tomatoes dry with kitchen paper, then slice them and place them on top of the filling, with the sun-dried tomatoes. Sprinkle with pepper and bake the tarts in the oven for 30 minutes.

Cool in the tins for about 15 minutes, and serve warm.

(pictured on pages 4/5)

RED CABBAGE WITH CHESTNUTS

Preparation time: 20 minutes + 3 hours cooking   Serves 4

1 tablespoon olive oil

15 g (½ oz) butter

50 g (2 oz) unsmoked bacon, de-rinded and chopped

1 onion, chopped

2 garlic cloves, crushed

450 g (15 oz) red cabbage, sliced finely

1 cooking apple, peeled and sliced

300 ml (½ pint) red wine and stock, mixed

Red cabbage is the perfect accompaniment to any game dish. With the addition of chestnuts, it is the ideal vegetable dish to serve with the Christmas turkey or indeed any festive game dish. If you cannot obtain fresh chestnuts, use dried chestnuts, reconstituted in water or wine.

Preheat the oven to Gas Mark 3/160°C/325°F. Heat the oil and butter in a large casserole and gently fry the bacon, onion and garlic until softened. Add the red cabbage and cook, stirring, for about 5 minutes. Add the remaining ingredients except the chestnuts, and bring to the boil. Cover and transfer to the oven. Cook for about 2 hours.

pinch of ground cloves
nutmeg
¼ teaspoon salt
pepper
12 fresh chestnuts

If using fresh chestnuts, make a small slit on the flat side with a sharp knife; roast them in a hot oven for 5 minutes, then peel off the two layers of outer skin. Stir the chestnuts into the red cabbage after the 2 hours, then cover and cook for a further 1 hour.

Remove from the oven, season to taste and serve. (This reheats very well the next day.)

AUBERGINE PROVENÇALE

Preparation time: 30 minutes + 1 hour 'salting'
+ 30–40 minutes cooking   Serves 4

1 large aubergine
2–3 tablespoons olive oil
2 garlic cloves, very finely chopped
40 g (1½ oz) cheese, grated
salt
For the tomato sauce:
1 tablespoon olive oil
1 onion, chopped
1 garlic clove, chopped
400 g (14 oz) can of tomatoes
a sprig of parsley
a sprig of thyme
salt and pepper

When I was au pair with a French family in Provence, Madame used to make this aubergine dish regularly. She would, of course, use fresh, Provence tomatoes, but cans of tomatoes are a great store-cupboard standby. A mixture of Gruyère and parmesan was used in Provence, but any strongly flavoured cheese will do.

Cut the aubergine into slices (about 1 cm/ ½-inch thick) and lay the slices on a plate. Sprinkle salt over them, cover with a piece of kitchen paper and leave for about an hour, to draw out any bitter juices.

For the tomato sauce, heat the oil in a saucepan and gently fry the onion and garlic until softened. Add the tomatoes and the herbs and cook, uncovered, for about 15–20 minutes. Remove any woody twigs of thyme. Sieve or purée the tomatoes, season to taste and reserve.

Wipe the aubergine slices dry with kitchen paper, then heat the oil in a large frying pan. Fry the aubergines on both sides (about 2–3 minutes each side) and drain on kitchen paper. Preheat the oven to Gas Mark 5/190°C/375°F. Place the aubergines in a lightly oiled ovenproof dish, top with the garlic, then spoon the tomato sauce over the top. Sprinkle over the grated cheese and place in the oven for about 15–20 minutes, until browned. Serve at once, with plenty of french bread.

PASTA AND GRAINS

PASTA WITH MUSHROOM AND CREAM SAUCE

Preparation time: 20 minutes + 35 minutes cooking
+ 30 minutes baking   Serves 4–6

50 g (2 oz) butter

2 garlic cloves, crushed

*500 g (1 lb) mixed
mushrooms, sliced thinly*

*375 g (12 oz) dried
macaroni, rigatoni or penne*

65 g (2½ oz) plain flour

300 ml (½ pint) milk

*142 ml (¼ pint) carton of
double cream*

*2 tablespoons freshly
chopped parsley*

*2 tablespoons freshly grated
parmesan cheese*

*a dash of truffle oil
(optional)*

salt and pepper

*My Italian friend Anna often cooks this creamy
mushroom dish for me, because I adore it. You can use
any type of mushroom – even wild ones such as ceps or
chanterelles. A dash of truffle oil (or even finely
chopped truffle) makes this dish even more aromatic.*

Heat the butter in a saucepan and fry the garlic
gently for 1 minute. Add the mushrooms and
cook for 15 minutes, over a low heat, stirring
occasionally. Season with salt.

Cook the dried pasta for 2 minutes less than
the packet instructions. Meanwhile, add the
flour to the mushrooms and stir well for 1
minute, then slowly add the milk and stir to
form a sauce. (This takes about 5–8 minutes.)
Remove the pan from the heat and stir in the
cream, parsley, parmesan cheese and pepper.
Taste for seasoning (add the truffle oil at this
stage, if used).

Preheat the oven to Gas Mark 4/180°C/
350°F. Drain the pasta well and immediately
mix into the mushroom sauce. Pour into a
buttered ovenproof dish and bake in the oven,
covered with oiled foil, for 20 minutes, then
uncovered for a further 10 minutes. Serve
piping hot, with a crisp salad.

CHICKEN LIVERS WITH PASTA AND GARLIC

Preparation time: 20 minutes + 15 minutes cooking   Serves 3–4

1 tablespoon olive oil

*250 g (8 oz) chicken
livers, thawed if frozen,
trimmed and halved*

*By cooking the chicken livers very quickly, at a high
heat, the result is rosy pink inside and crispy outside.
The garlic and lemon make the sauce powerful and
full of flavour. I prefer to use home-made pasta for
this, but dried tagliatelle is also good.*

250–275 ml (8–9 fl oz) chicken stock	Preheat the oven to Gas Mark 3/160°C/325°F. Heat the oil in a large frying–pan and add the livers when it is very hot. Fry for 2 minutes on a high heat. Remove the livers and drain them on kitchen paper. Place on a plate and rest them in the warm oven.
3 garlic cloves, crushed	
25 g (1 oz) parmesan cheese, grated	
3–4 tablespoons double cream	

Pour the stock into the frying–pan and simmer to reduce the liquid by half. Add the garlic, parmesan, cream, lemon zest and juice, and reduce until thickened. (This should take about 5 minutes.) Meanwhile cook the pasta, according to the packet instructions. Drain well and toss in a little olive oil.

grated zest and juice of 1 large lemon	
375–425 g (12–14 oz) fresh or dried tagliatelle	
olive oil, to toss	
salt and pepper	
fresh parsley or chervil, chopped roughly, to garnish	

Season the sauce to taste. Place the pasta in a large warmed bowl, top with the chicken livers and pour the sauce all around. Garnish with chopped parsley or chervil.

COLD LASAGNE OF SMOKED SALMON, PARSLEY AND TOMATO

Preparation time: 45 minutes + 30 minutes cooking + overnight chilling

Serves 5–6

For the tomato sauce:

The thought of a cold lasagne might not inspire everyone, but this is a lasagne with a difference. It is a succulent dish, full of bold flavours which work together beautifully. The best results come from using fresh lasagne, but if you buy dried 'pre-cooked' lasagne, you must boil it (until 'al dente') before assembling it in the dish. Serve it with a lightly dressed crisp salad and some warm french bread.

1 tablespoon olive oil	
1 onion, chopped	
1 large garlic clove, chopped	
1 small celery stick, chopped	
1 small carrot, chopped finely	
400 g (14 oz) can of tomatoes	
4–5 basil leaves	
salt and pepper	

Brush a lasagne dish (big enough to accommodate 2 lasagne sheets per layer – about 20 × 25 cm/8 × 10 inches) with olive oil.

For the parsley sauce:

To make the tomato sauce, heat the oil in a saucepan and fry the onion, garlic, celery and carrot for 3–4 minutes. Add the tomatoes and their juices with the basil, and cook uncovered over a moderate heat for about 20 minutes until the vegetables are soft. Pour into a food processor or liquidiser and purée until smooth. Season to taste, and allow to cool.

40 g (1½ oz) fresh parsley, stalks removed	

3 garlic cloves, crushed

150 ml (¼ pint) extra-virgin olive oil

salt and pepper

For the lasagne:

extra-virgin olive oil, for brushing

6 sheets of lasagne, cooked and drained

250 g (8 oz) smoked salmon, cut into slivers

150 g (5 oz) young leaf spinach, sorrel or rocket, shredded

salt and pepper

To make the parsley sauce, put the parsley and garlic in a food processor and process until combined. Slowly add the oil, with the machine running, until you have a thick sauce. Season to taste.

To assemble, place 2 sheets of cooked lasagne on the bottom of the dish. Spoon the parsley sauce over the lasagne, spreading it out well. Top with half of the smoked salmon. Place another 2 sheets of lasagne on the salmon, then spoon over the tomato sauce. Top with the remaining smoked salmon, then roughly shred the spinach (or sorrel or rocket) and place in an even layer over the salmon. Season lightly with salt and pepper. Finish by placing the last 2 sheets of lasagne on top and brush them with olive oil. Cover with clingfilm and refrigerate overnight. Remove the dish from the refrigerator 1 hour before serving.

FRESH PASTA WITH LEMON AND CREAM

Preparation time: 30 minutes + 1–1¼ hours 'resting' + 5 minutes cooking

Serves 3–4

For the pasta:

250 g (8 oz) strong white flour

2 large eggs (size 1–2)

1 teaspoon salt

1 teaspoon olive oil

For the sauce:

142 ml (¼ pint) carton of double cream

zest of 1 large lemon

pepper

3 tablespoons freshly grated parmesan cheese

This simple yet delicious pasta sauce should be accompanied by fresh pasta, either bought or home-made. I always roll out the dough in my pasta machine, but it is quite simple without one: simply roll out the dough as thinly as possible and cut into the required shape. The easiest way to cut tagliatelle is to roll up the thin dough into a cylinder shape, then cut into even widths. Shake these coils into individual noodle shapes.

For the pasta, place all the ingredients except the oil in a food processor. Process briefly, then add the oil. Process until the mixture comes together to form a ball. (If necessary add a tiny dribble more oil, until it comes together.) Turn out the mixture, knead briefly until it is smooth and wrap in clingfilm. Let it rest in the refrigerator for 30 minutes.

Cut the dough into 4 pieces, then roll each piece 5 or 6 times through the widest setting on your pasta machine, folding and 'half-turning' it each time. Then roll it through the other rollers, until the penultimate setting. (The last setting is the finest, but the pasta tends to stick when cut.) Lay out the 4 sheets of pasta to dry a little, for about 30–45 minutes, then pass them through the tagliatelle cutters. You can either cook them straight away or hang them on a pasta hanger or chair back to dry for about 30 minutes (then refrigerate until needed).

For the sauce, heat the cream and lemon zest in a saucepan over a low heat, until hot and thick, then season well with plenty of pepper. Meanwhile, cook the pasta in boiling salted water for no more than 1 minute if freshly made, or about 3 minutes if dried briefly. Drain well and toss immediately into the sauce. Add the parmesan, stir well to coat, and serve at once in warmed bowls.

BARLEY RISOTTO

Preparation time: 20 minutes + 40 minutes cooking
Serves 3–4 as a main course, 5–6 as an accompaniment

¼ teaspoon saffron strands
300 ml (½ pint) light vegetable or chicken stock
50 g (2 oz) unsalted butter
1 onion, chopped finely
2 garlic cloves, chopped finely
175 g (6 oz) large flat or button mushrooms, sliced
200 g (7 oz) pearl barley
½ teaspoon salt
pepper
chopped fresh parsley, to garnish

Barley makes an unusual alternative to rice in a risotto, and never loses its 'bite' as some rice dishes tend to do. I like to use saffron to add both flavour and colour, but it is not essential – an extra tablespoon of freshly chopped parsley will add a pleasing colour contrast. This is good as a vegetarian main course or as an accompaniment to any game dish.

Preheat the oven to Gas Mark 3/160°C/325°F. Soak the saffron strands in the stock for 10 minutes.

Melt the butter in a flameproof casserole; add the onion and garlic and fry gently for 4–5 minutes. Add the mushrooms and cook for about 3 minutes, then add the barley and stir well to coat with the butter. Add the stock (with the saffron), salt and pepper and bring to the boil, stirring well. Remove the pan from the heat, cover with a tight-fitting lid and transfer to the oven. Cook for 35–40 minutes, until all the liquid is absorbed.

Remove from the oven, fluff up the grains with a fork and serve at once, garnished with freshly chopped parsley.

KEDGEREE WITH DILL

Preparation time: 30 minutes + 35 minutes cooking   Serves 4

2 hard-boiled eggs, quartered

375 g (12 oz) undyed smoked haddock, cooked and flaked

250 g (8 oz) cooked rice (100 g/3½ oz uncooked rice yields this cooked weight)

juice of 1 lemon

a pinch of chilli powder (Cayenne pepper)

2–3 tablespoons chopped fresh dill

142 ml (¼ pint) carton of single cream

50 g (2 oz) butter

salt

fresh dill, to garnish

Kedgeree for breakfast does nothing for me, I'm afraid, but a well-cooked kedgeree for a light lunch or supper dish is delightful. The addition of freshly chopped dill adds a fresh taste and a good green colour. Take care to mix the ingredients gently.

Preheat the oven to Gas Mark 4/180°C/350°F. Mix together the eggs, fish and rice. Add the lemon juice, salt, chilli powder and dill. Stir in the cream, then spoon the mixture into a well-buttered ovenproof dish. Dot the remaining butter over the top, cover with a lid and cook in the preheated oven for about 35 minutes.

Garnish with a sprig of fresh dill and serve piping hot.

TAGLIATELLE WITH SMOKED TROUT, CHIVES AND CRÈME FRAÎCHE

Preparation time: 15 minutes + 1 hour 'standing'
+ 15 minutes cooking   Serves 4–6 as a starter

125 g (4 oz) smoked trout
200 ml (7 fl oz) carton of crème fraîche
2 tablespoons chopped fresh chives
250 g (8 oz) tagliatelle
25 g (1 oz) unsalted butter
pepper
chopped fresh chives, to garnish

I love the combination of smoked fish with pasta. Slices of smoked trout are not only cheaper than smoked salmon, but they also have a more subtle flavour. The crème fraîche adds a sharpness to the creamy sauce and the chives give a wonderful colour. Dried or fresh pasta can be used.

Cut the trout into small pieces (it is easier to use scissors) and place in a small saucepan with the crème fraîche and chives. Leave to stand for about an hour.

Cook the tagliatelle until 'al dente' (according to the packet instructions), drain well and toss in the butter. Add plenty of pepper.

While the pasta is cooking, heat the sauce in the saucepan over a low heat until hot, but not boiling. Pour the sauce over the freshly cooked pasta, toss well and serve at once, in warmed bowls, garnished with chives.

RÖSTI OF PASTA

Preparation time: 5 minutes + 25 minutes cooking   Serves 4

175 g (6 oz) dried spaghetti
½ teaspoon salt
1 tablespoon olive oil
pepper
To serve:
extra-virgin olive oil
shavings of fresh parmesan cheese

These are little rounds of freshly cooked pasta, tossed in olive oil, piled into muffin rings and fried. The result is a crispy golden exterior and a soft pasta interior. I think they are best made with spaghetti, but tagliatelle is also good. Serve them with a roast meat such as lamb, rabbit or beef.

Cook the pasta in plenty of boiling water with the salt, until 'al dente' (according to the packet instructions). Drain well and toss in ½ tablespoon of the oil. Add plenty of pepper.

In a large frying-pan, position four oiled muffin rings (8 cm/3 inches; you could use metal biscuit cutters). Add a little olive oil to

each ring, spreading it out with kitchen paper. When the oil is very hot, spoon in the cooked pasta, pressing it down to pack in well (Fig. 1). (You may have to do this in 2 batches.) After 3 minutes on a high heat, carefully turn both ring and pasta over using two fish slices, one positioned on top of the ring and the other slid underneath (Fig. 2). Continue cooking over a high heat for another 2 minutes, then remove the pan from the heat. Leave to rest in the pan for 2–3 minutes (the heat of the rings will keep them hot). Very carefully, slide a fish slice under and remove them to a warm plate. Taking care not to burn your fingers, remove the rings.

Drizzle with some extra-virgin olive oil and serve with a shaving of fresh parmesan.

SPAGHETTI WITH SORREL PESTO

Preparation time: 20 minutes + 12 minutes cooking   Serves 4–6

200 g (7 oz) young sorrel, spinach or rocket leaves, stalks removed

2 garlic cloves, chopped

3 tablespoons freshly grated parmesan cheese

2 tablespoons pine kernels

½ teaspoon salt

125–150 ml (4–5 fl oz) extra-virgin olive oil

300 g (10 oz) dried spaghetti, vermicelli or capellini

toasted pine kernels, to garnish

Sorrel has a wonderfully sharp, almost lemony flavour which makes it an excellent foil for fish dishes; it also makes a delicious soup and a piquant accompaniment to pasta. In order to retain its brilliant green colour, it should never be overheated, or it will turn to a rusty brown. This pesto recipe means that its lively colour is retained, as it is mixed with hot pasta at the last minute, and not actually cooked. The pesto is also an interesting addition to any vegetable soup, but it must be stirred in immediately prior to serving.

To make the pesto, place the sorrel, garlic, parmesan, pine kernels and salt in a food processor or a blender and process until the mixture is finely chopped. With the motor running, slowly pour in sufficient oil to give a thick sauce, with the consistency of mayonnaise.

(continued on page 54)

Tagliatelle with Smoked Trout, Chives and Crème Fraîche

Rösti of Pasta

Spaghetti with Sorrel Pesto

(At this stage, it can be stored in a screw-top jar for several weeks in the refrigerator; it also freezes well.)

Cook the pasta according to the packet instructions, then drain. Pour the pesto over the pasta and toss through. Garnish with toasted pine kernels and serve at once, in a warmed bowl, with some warm Italian bread such as ciabatta.

CHICKEN LIVER AND RICE TIMBALE

Preparation time: 25 minutes + 1½ hours cooking
+ 20 minutes cooling + 10–15 minutes resting   Serves 5–6

For the risotto:

40 g (1½ oz) butter

1 onion, chopped finely

250 g (8 oz) chicken livers, thawed if frozen, trimmed and chopped

grated zest of 1 lemon

325 g (11 oz) risotto rice

1.2 litres (2 pints) hot chicken stock

salt and pepper

For the timbale:

3 tablespoons fresh white breadcrumbs

150 g (5 oz) mozzarella cheese, sliced

2 hard-boiled eggs, quartered

2 tablespoons freshly grated parmesan cheese

parmesan cheese, to serve

This is really a chicken liver risotto, layered with mozzarella and eggs, and baked in the oven. It is then turned out, like a cake, to show the golden crust which has formed from a mixture of breadcrumbs and parmesan cheese. It can be served with a fresh tomato sauce, such as the one given on page 46.

To make the risotto, heat the butter in a saucepan and gently fry the onion for about 3 minutes. Add the livers, lemon zest, salt and pepper and fry for about 3 minutes, until the livers are browned. Add the rice, stirring well to coat with the butter, and then cook for about 3 minutes. Gradually add the stock, ladle by ladle, until all the liquid is absorbed and the rice is tender, stirring frequently to prevent sticking. (This takes about 20–25 minutes.) Season to taste and leave to cool for about 20 minutes.

Preheat the oven to Gas Mark 4/180°C/ 350°F. Liberally butter a deep, round, ovenproof dish (about 1.75 litres/3 pints) and sprinkle about half the breadcrumbs over the buttered surface. Spoon about two-thirds of the risotto into the dish, pressing well down and around the sides, to make a hollow in the middle. Arrange the mozzarella and eggs in the middle, then spoon over the remaining risotto. Press everything down fairly firmly. Sprinkle the remaining breadcrumbs and the parmesan cheese over the top and bake in the oven for 1 hour.

Remove from the oven and allow to rest for about 10–15 minutes, then carefully invert on to a warmed plate. Offer extra parmesan cheese with the dish.

RICE BALLS WITH CHEESE

Preparation time: 20 minutes + 30 minutes toasting + 1–2 hours chilling + 25 minutes cooking   Makes about 25 balls

For the risotto:

25 g (1 oz) butter

1 tablespoon olive oil

1 onion, chopped finely

250 g (8 oz) risotto rice

900 ml (1½ pints) hot chicken stock

salt and pepper

For the rice balls:

75 g (3 oz) fresh breadcrumbs

1 egg, beaten

75 g (3 oz) fresh parmesan cheese, grated

2 tablespoons freshly chopped herbs, e.g. parsley, marjoram or thyme

oil for deep-frying

These are in fact deep-fried balls of risotto mixed with egg and parmesan cheese. They are best eaten warm, and are good to serve with drinks or to take on a picnic. Risotto rice is widely available and produces better results for risotto than using long-grain.

To make the risotto, heat the butter and oil in a pan and add the onion; cook for 2 minutes. Add the rice and, stirring to coat, cook for another 2 minutes. Gradually add the stock, a little at a time, until all of the liquid is absorbed and the rice is tender (about 20 minutes). Season to taste. Leave to cool, either for an hour or overnight.

Toast the breadcrumbs in a warm oven until dried (about 30 minutes). Mix the egg, parmesan and herbs into the risotto mixture. With dampened hands, roll the mixture into walnut-size balls. Roll these in the breadcrumbs and chill for 1–2 hours in the refrigerator.

Preheat a deep-fryer to hot (about 180°C/350°F) or heat the oil in a heavy-bottomed pan. Deep-fry the balls for about 5–6 minutes in batches, until they are crisp and golden brown. Drain on kitchen paper before serving.

ORANGE AND CORIANDER COUSCOUS

Preparation time: 10 minutes + 20–25 minutes cooking
+ 20–25 minutes 'standing'   Serves 8

500 ml (18 fl oz) carton of
freshly squeezed orange
juice

300 ml (½ pint) water

1 small onion, chopped
finely

2 garlic cloves, crushed

50 g (2 oz) butter

1 teaspoon salt

500 g (1 lb) couscous

4 tablespoons coarsely
chopped fresh coriander
leaves

coriander leaves, to garnish

*This couscous dish makes a welcome change from the
usual accompaniment of boiled rice with so many
ethnic dishes. Nowadays most packets of couscous are
'precooked', so they only need to be steamed briefly.
The subtle flavour of orange is enhanced with the
freshly chopped coriander – it goes well with fish,
meat or vegetarian dishes.*

Place the orange juice, water, onion and garlic
in a pan; bring to the boil and boil rapidly for
20–25 minutes until reduced to 600 ml/1 pint.

Heat the butter and salt gently in a large
frying-pan and, when the butter has melted,
add the couscous and stir until the grains are
well coated. Add the reduced orange juice and
stir well. Turn off the heat, cover with two
double tea towels (to steam the couscous) and
set aside for about 20–25 minutes.

Remove the couscous and fluff up the grains
with a fork. Season to taste and add the coarsely
chopped coriander.

Garnish with some fresh coriander leaves.

*Rice Balls with Cheese
Orange and Coriander Couscous*

FISH AND SHELLFISH

TROUT WITH FENNEL AND ORANGE

Preparation time: 10 minutes + 12–14 minutes grilling   Serves 2

2 trout, weighing about
300 g (10 oz) each,
cleaned and scaled,

1½ tablespoons olive oil

2 oranges

2 tablespoons fennel leaves

salt

orange slices, to garnish

The aniseed taste of fresh fennel leaves permeates this fish dish and combines with the orange and olive oil to give the trout a distinctive flavour. The cooking juices are poured over the fish at the end, as a sauce; you need plenty of good crusty bread to mop up the plate. A crisp salad of sliced fennel bulb mixed with orange segments and some watercress is an ideal accompaniment.

Wash and dry the fish well. Sprinkle the insides with a little salt. Make 2 slashes in each side (to ensure even cooking), and lay in a flame-proof dish. Brush all over with the olive oil. Heat the grill to moderate.

Cut 2 slices from the oranges; cut these in two and place them into each fish's cavity. Then fill the fish with the fennel leaves. Squeeze the juice from the oranges over both fish, and place under the grill. Grill for about 6–7 minutes on each side, depending on the size, and baste a couple of times with the juices.

Transfer the fish carefully, with a fish slice, on to a serving plate, and pour the pan juices over them. Garnish with orange slices.

PRAWNS WITH COCONUT SAUCE

Preparation time: 15 minutes + 20 minutes cooking   Serves 4

2 tablespoons olive oil

1 onion, chopped finely

1 garlic clove, crushed

5 tablespoons creamed
tomatoes

This is a very mild dish of prawns with coconut, tomatoes and parsley. I like to 'liven' it up at the end by the addition of some chilli powder. Serve with buttered rice and a fresh tomato salad.

Heat the oil in a saucepan and fry the onion and garlic gently for 5 minutes.

Add the tomatoes and parsley and cook for a

| | further 5 minutes. Add the coconut and stir |

3 tablespoons chopped fresh parsley

125 g (4 oz) creamed coconut, chopped finely

500 g (1 lb) peeled prawns, thawed if frozen, drained

3–4 tablespoons water

a pinch of chilli powder (Cayenne pepper)

salt and pepper

chopped fresh parsley, to garnish

further 5 minutes. Add the coconut and stir carefully to blend. Add the prawns and water and cook gently for about 10 minutes, stirring frequently to prevent sticking. Season to taste with salt, pepper and a pinch of chilli powder. Serve hot, with a sprinkling of parsley.

SCALLOPS WITH ORANGE AND THYME

Preparation time: 20 minutes + 2 hours chilling
+ 10 minutes cooking   Serves 4

125 g (4 oz) unsalted butter, softened

4 tablespoons fresh thyme leaves

grated zest of 1 large orange

750 g (1½ lb) scallops, cleaned

salt and pepper

thyme sprigs, to garnish

Scallops are my favourite seafood. I love to serve them very simply fried or seared on a cast-iron griddle, with the lightest and most simple of sauces. In this recipe, they are cooked in a butter flavoured with thyme and orange, then served with a little of the butter on top. It is a good idea to serve plain boiled rice with them; at the last minute, I like to pour off any pan juices (which still contain the flavoured butter) into the rice and stir.

To make the butter, place the butter, thyme and orange zest in a food processor and blend until well combined (or chop the thyme and orange zest, place in a bowl and beat together with the butter until smooth). Remove 3–4 teaspoons of the flavoured butter for frying. Shape the rest into a log shape, roll tightly in clingfilm and refrigerate for 1–2 hours. When solid, remove the clingfilm and slice the butter very thinly into round discs.

If the scallops are fairly thick, cut them horizontally, almost, but not quite, in two. Season with salt and pepper.

59

Heat the reserved butter in a large frying-pan until very hot. Fry the scallops for no more than 1½ minutes on each side (smaller ones can take 1 minute each side), then transfer to warmed serving plates. (Do not overcrowd the pan; do them in batches if necessary.) Place a thin disc of the butter on top of each scallop, decorate with the thyme and serve at once.

SALMON FILLET WITH BASIL CREAM SAUCE

Preparation time: 15 minutes + 5 minutes cooking   Serves 4

4 × salmon tail fillets, weighing about 175 g (6 oz) each

olive oil, for brushing

1 tablespoon pesto sauce

142 ml (¼ pint) carton of double cream

1 tablespoon lemon juice

fresh basil, to garnish

Salmon and basil go together remarkably well. I like to serve this with some pasta, tossed in olive oil.

Preheat the grill to high, brush the salmon fillets with olive oil and lay them in a flameproof dish. In a small saucepan, mix the pesto and cream and bring slowly to the boil.

Meanwhile, grill the salmon for about 2–3 minutes, depending on the thickness, turn and cook for a further 2–3 minutes. (Test by inserting a knife to check whether it is done.)

Remove the sauce from the heat as soon as it boils, stir in the lemon juice, and serve it with the grilled salmon. Garnish with fresh basil.

CRAB QUICHE

Preparation time: 25 minutes + 1½ hours 'resting' + 15 minutes 'blind' baking + 30 minutes baking   Serves 6

For the pastry:

250 g (8 oz) plain flour, sifted

¼ teaspoon salt

grated zest of 1 orange

125 g (4 oz) unsalted butter, cubed

Crab is a great favourite of mine. I like it in sandwiches, soups, soufflés and, probably best of all, freshly boiled and eaten with some good bread and butter. This recipe is for a pastry case with a creamy filling of crabmeat (I like a mixture of the white and brown meat), flavoured with lemon and chilli powder. It is good served for lunch, with a fennel or nasturtium salad, or a garlic-laden mayonnaise.

Salmon fillet with Basil Cream Sauce

1 egg yolk

1–2 teaspoons lemon juice

For the filling:

375 g (12 oz) fresh
crabmeat, (or frozen,
thawed and well drained, or
canned, very well drained)

3 eggs, beaten

juice of ½ lemon

a pinch of chilli powder
(Cayenne pepper)

142 ml (¼ pint) carton of
double cream

salt

To make the pastry, place the flour, salt and orange zest in a food processor. Add the butter and process briefly until the mixture resembles fine breadcrumbs. Add the egg yolk and 1 teaspoon of the lemon juice and process until the mixture forms a ball. (Add the extra lemon juice if necessary.) Wrap in clingfilm and refrigerate for about 30 minutes.

Roll the pastry out to line a 23 cm (9-inch) flan tin. Prick the base with a fork and leave to rest in the refrigerator for about 1 hour. Preheat the oven to Gas Mark 6/200°C/400°F. Bake the pastry case blind (with baking parchment and beans) for 10 minutes. Remove the baking parchment and beans, and bake for a further 5 minutes. Remove and cool slightly. Reduce the oven temperature to Gas Mark 5/190°C/375°F.

To make the filling, mix together the crabmeat, eggs, lemon juice, chilli powder (Cayenne pepper) and salt. Gently stir in the cream. Pour the mixture carefully into the pastry case and bake in the oven for 25 – 30 minutes, until it is set. Cool in the tin, then carefully remove on to a serving plate and serve warm, in wedges.

HAKE WITH A CORIANDER CRUST

Preparation time: 15 minutes + 15 minutes baking   Serves 4

4–5 tablespoons fresh
coriander leaves

50 g (2 oz) walnut pieces

2 garlic cloves, crushed

1 tablespoon lime juice

25 g (1 oz) fresh parmesan
cheese, grated

90–125 ml (3–4 fl oz)
extra-virgin olive oil

4 × hake cutlets, weighing
about 150–175 g (5–6 oz)
each

Hake is a member of the cod family, and has a rather soft flesh. Care must be taken, therefore, not to overcook it. If hake cutlets are unavailable, cod steaks work very well. I like to accompany this dish with orange-flavoured couscous (page 56). Fried capers make a delicious garnish.

Preheat the oven to Gas Mark 5/190°C/375°F. Place the coriander leaves, walnuts, garlic, lime juice and parmesan in a food processor or blender and purée briefly; slowly add enough oil to give a thick paste consistency. Season to taste with salt and pepper.

Place the hake cutlets side by side in an oiled,

salt and pepper

sprigs of coriander, to garnish

shallow ovenproof dish; season them with salt and pepper. Brush with olive oil, then divide the coriander mixture between the cutlets and spread over each. Bake in the top half of the oven for about 15 minutes, depending on the thickness of the cutlets (thick ones take about 18 minutes). Test after 12 minutes with the tip of a sharp knife, to check whether they are cooked. Carefully remove them with a fish slice and serve, with any juices from the dish poured over them. Garnish with a sprig of coriander.

STIR-FRY OF SQUID WITH LEMON GRASS AND GARLIC

Preparation time: 25 minutes   Serves 2

1 tablespoon sunflower oil

2 fresh stalks of lemon grass, tough outer layers removed, chopped finely

2–3 garlic cloves, chopped

1 baby leek, sliced thinly

3–4 spring onions, sliced thinly

200 g (7 oz) cleaned squid tubes (with tentacles), sliced into 1 cm (½-inch) rings

1 tablespoon chilli sauce

1 tablespoon light soy sauce

1 tablespoon Thai fish sauce (Nam Pla) (optional)

4 tablespoons chopped fresh coriander leaves

coriander leaves, to garnish

I like squid when it is stir-fried, as there is no hint of the rubbery texture which overcooking can produce. Lemon grass, garlic, chilli and soy sauce give this dish the flavours of the East, which can be subtle, even when hot and spicy.

Heat the oil in a large frying-pan or wok until very hot. Add the lemon grass and garlic and fry, stirring all the time, for half a minute. Add the leek and spring onions, and continue stirring over a high heat for 2 minutes.

Add the squid and stir-fry for another 1 minute. Add the chilli sauce, soy sauce and fish sauce (if used), and continue cooking for another 1 minute. Add the chopped coriander, stir and serve at once, garnished with coriander leaves.

Crab Quiche

Hake with
a Coriander Crust

*Stir-fry of Squid with
Lemon Grass and Garlic*

FISH IN FOIL PARCELS

Preparation time: 20 minutes + 20 minutes cooking   Serves 4

2 baby leeks, sliced very thinly

4 fillets of white fish, weighing about 150–175 g (5–6 oz) each

125 g (4 oz) peeled prawns, thawed if frozen

1 tablespoon grated fresh root ginger

zest of 1 large lemon

4 tablespoons lemon juice

40 g (1½ oz) butter, melted

salt and pepper

The flavours of ginger and lemon make this baked fish taste refreshingly sharp and delicious. You can use any skinned fillets of white fish, such as cod or haddock. If the fillet is a long shape, cut it in half and place one on top of the other, in the parcel: the overall shape should be square. I like to serve this with tiny new potatoes or crusty bread, to 'dunk' into the buttery juices.

Preheat the oven to Gas Mark 6/200°C/400°F. Cut out 4 squares of thick foil, about 33 cm (13 inches). Place a bed of leeks in the centre of each, then lay the fish fillets on top. Divide the prawns between the four parcels, then sprinkle over the ginger and lemon zest. Season well with salt and pepper. Pour over the lemon juice and melted butter. Gather up the edges (Fig. 1) and make into a parcel, by folding the edges tightly together (Fig. 2). Place on a baking sheet, and bake in the oven for 15–20 minutes, until cooked. (Check after 12 minutes, by opening a corner of the parcel; test with the point of a knife and reseal if not yet ready.) To serve, place each parcel on a plate and either fold back the edges of the foil or let your guests have the treat of opening it themselves.

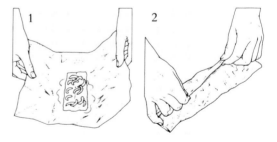

SALMON STEAK WITH A YELLOW PEPPER SAUCE

Preparation time: 20 minutes + 25 minutes cooking   Serves 4

3 tablespoons olive oil

1 onion, chopped finely

3 yellow peppers, de-seeded and chopped

50 g (2 oz) butter

3 garlic cloves, crushed

4 salmon steaks, weighing about 175 g (6 oz) each

salt and pepper

The sweetness of the yellow pepper should be balanced by plenty of freshly ground pepper on the salmon; cover the fish as you would for a peppered steak. The sauce can be made in advance and reheated.

Heat 2 tablespoons of the oil in a large pan, and fry the onion and peppers gently for about 15 minutes, or until softened.

Transfer to a food processor, with the remaining oil, and process until smooth. Season to taste, and place in a small saucepan.

Heat the butter and garlic in a large frying-pan. Sprinkle plenty of pepper and a little salt over the salmon steaks, and fry them in the garlic butter for about 3 minutes on each side, depending on the thickness. Reheat the sauce gently for a couple of minutes, if necessary.

Place the salmon on to warmed plates and pour the sauce beside or over the fish.

67

MEAT, POULTRY AND GAME

ROAST VENISON WITH REDCURRANT JELLY

Preparation time: 15 minutes + 30–60 minutes cooking
+ 15 minutes 'resting'   Serves 4–6

50 g (2 oz) butter

2 teaspoons redcurrant jelly

*1–1.75 kg (2–4 lb)
venison joint*

pepper

For the sauce:

3 tablespoons red wine

*2 teaspoons raspberry or
other fruit vinegar*

*300 ml (½ pint) game
stock or beef stock*

1 teaspoon redcurrant jelly

salt and pepper

*This venison dish makes such a welcome change for
the Sunday roast. The flavour of farmed venison is
not too 'gamey', so the children also love it. I like to
use the sirloin, but a haunch or shoulder are also
suitable for this fast roasting method. It is very
important with such a lean meat as venison to
undercook the joint slightly, then let it rest, covered
in foil, for at least 15 minutes. The result is a moist,
evenly-cooked, medium-rare joint. Any further
cooking will make the meat dry and tough, so this
joint and roasting method is not suitable if you prefer
well-done meat.*

Preheat the oven to Gas Mark 8/230°C/450°F.
In a large frying-pan, melt the butter with the
redcurrant jelly until very hot. Add the meat
and quickly brown all over. Carefully lift the
joint from the pan and place it in a roasting tin.
Pour over the butter from the pan. Season the
meat with pepper. Place the roasting tin in the
oven. Cook for about 30–40 minutes per 1 kg
(2 lb); the result will be medium-rare, after
resting. (If you want it rare, cook for 20
minutes per 1 kg/2 lb.) Baste a couple of times
during cooking; cover it with foil after about 20
minutes to keep it moist.

Remove the roasting tin from the oven and
transfer the joint to a carving board. Cover
tightly with double foil and rest for at least 15
minutes. Carve into slices once rested.

Pour off any excess fat from the roasting tin,
then place the tin directly on to the stove, over a
high heat. Add the red wine and vinegar and,
stirring to scrape up all the flavours from the
tin, boil for 1–2 minutes. Add the stock and the

*Roast Venison with
Redcurrant Jelly*

jelly and cook over a high heat, stirring all the time. After 3–4 minutes, the liquid will have reduced to a sauce-like consistency. Season to taste then sieve (to remove any caramelised bits from the base of the tin) and serve with the meat.

GUINNESS BEEF WITH PICKLED WALNUTS

Preparation time: 45 minutes + 3¼ hours cooking   Serves 6

1 large onion, chopped

3 garlic cloves, chopped

50 g (2 oz) butter

2 tablespoons olive oil

1 leek, chopped

½ swede, chopped

2 carrots, sliced

1 kg (2 lb) rump steak, cubed

2 tablespoons seasoned flour

2 sprigs of fresh thyme

¼ teaspoon ground mace

600 ml (1 pint) Guinness or Irish Stout

250 g (8 oz) mushrooms, sliced thickly

grated zest and juice of 1 small orange

8 pickled walnuts, drained and halved

salt and pepper

chopped fresh parsley, to serve

This hearty casserole can be made with any stout – the darker the better. Be sure to drain the walnuts from their pickling liquid, or the result will be too vinegary. I like to serve this with mashed potato or a mixture of creamed parsnip with potato.

Preheat the oven to Gas Mark 2/150°C/300°F. In a large flameproof casserole, gently fry the onions and garlic in half the butter and half the oil for 10 minutes. Remove with a slotted spoon, then add the leek, swede and carrots, and brown for about 5 minutes. Remove and add to the onions and garlic.

Toss the meat in the seasoned flour and brown in the remaining butter and oil. (It is better to do it in batches, so that you do not crowd the pan.) Once all the meat has been browned, return it with the vegetables to the casserole and add the thyme, mace, salt, pepper and Guinness. Bring to the boil, then tightly cover with foil and a lid and transfer to a low shelf in the oven. Cook for 2½ hours, stirring a couple of times.

Add the mushrooms, then cook for a further 30 minutes. Add the orange zest and juice, and the walnuts. Stir in gently, so that the walnuts do not break up. Return to the oven for another 15 minutes, then season to taste and serve, sprinkled with freshly chopped parsley.

PORK WITH PRUNES

Preparation time: 25 minutes + 1¼ hours cooking   Serves 4

2 tablespoons olive oil

25 g (1 oz) butter

1 kg (2 lb) boneless pork shoulder, trimmed and cut into cubes

1 large onion, chopped finely

1 garlic clove, crushed

rind of 1 orange, pared thinly

2 cloves

2 fresh sage leaves

500 ml (18 fl oz) dry cider

125 g (4 oz) pitted prunes

1 tablespoon quince jelly or apple jelly

salt and pepper

This is a German-inspired recipe, but it is not as heavy as some popular German dishes can be, because the juices are not thickened by flour: they are boiled until they are reduced, and then sweetened with quince or apple jelly.

Preheat the oven to Gas Mark 3/160°C/325°F. Heat the oil and butter in a large flameproof casserole and brown the pork, in batches, on all sides. Remove with a slotted spoon, then fry the onion and garlic until softened.

Return the meat to the pan, and add the orange rind, cloves, sage leaves and cider. Bring to the boil, then cover and transfer to the oven for 30 minutes. Add the prunes and cook for a further 30 minutes, or until the pork is tender.

Using a slotted spoon, transfer the pork, prunes and onions to a plate. Discard the rind, cloves and sage. Skim off any fat from the liquid. On the top of the stove, bring the liquid to the boil and reduce, uncovered, over a high heat, for about 5–10 minutes, until syrupy. Reduce the heat, add the jelly and stir until it dissolves. Season to taste and return the meat, prunes and onions to the pan. Reheat gently, and then serve.

Guinness Beef with Pickled Walnuts

Pork with Prunes

Lamb with Olive Paste

LAMB WITH OLIVE PASTE

Preparation time: 40 minutes + 15–20 minutes cooking   Serves 4

For the olive paste:

2 garlic cloves, crushed

20 large black olives, stoned

50 g (2 oz) canned anchovy fillets, drained

50 g (2 oz) canned tuna fish in oil, drained

2 tablespoons capers, drained

1 teaspoon Dijon mustard

juice of ½ lemon

125–175 ml (4–6 fl oz) olive oil

For the lamb:

75 g (3 oz) unsalted butter

8 small boneless lamb leg steaks, weighing about 75 g (3 oz) each

8 sheets of filo pastry, thawed if frozen

2 teaspoons sesame seeds

salt and pepper

The olive paste is my version of the Provençal tapenade, which is delicious spread on warm toast.

To make the olive paste, place all the ingredients except the oil, in a food processor or blender and whizz together until smooth. Slowly add sufficient oil to give a thick paste of spreading consistency. Store in a screw-top jar (where it will keep for 3–4 weeks).

Preheat the oven to Gas Mark 6/200°C/400°F. Melt 15 g (½ oz) of the butter in a frying-pan until hot, then brown the lamb steaks on all sides for no more than one minute. Season them and leave them to cool on kitchen paper.

Melt 50 g (2 oz) of the butter, then spread out 1 sheet of filo pastry on a work surface, and brush it with some butter. Place a second sheet on top, and brush with more butter. Place one of the lamb steaks in the middle and spread with a layer (about ½ tablespoon) of the olive paste, then top with another lamb steak (Fig. 1). Wrap up the pastry like a parcel (Fig. 2), tucking the ends underneath (Fig. 3). Place on a buttered baking sheet, while you repeat the operation three times more.

Melt the remaining butter and brush it over the tops of the parcels; then sprinkle them with sesame seeds. Bake in the preheated oven for about 12–15 minutes, or until the meat is just cooked (but still pink) and the pastry golden brown. Serve at once.

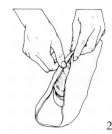

PHEASANT BREAST WITH MANGO SAUCE

Preparation time: 30 minutes + 1 hour chilling
+ 15 minutes cooking

Serves 8

For the sauce:

2 ripe mangoes

juice of ½ lime

284 ml (½ pint) carton of
double cream

1 × 340 g (11 oz) jar of
mango chutney, any large
chunks of mango mashed
with a fork

For the pheasant:

8 pheasant breasts

2 tablespoons olive oil

25 g (1 oz) butter

salt and pepper

slices of fresh ripe mango,
to serve

*This sounds rather an improbable combination, but
in fact the strong flavour of pheasant matches the
sweetness of fresh mango and mango chutney
remarkably well. If you cannot buy pheasant breasts,
buy 4 pheasants and, with a sharp knife, cut away
the breasts, holding the knife as close to the backbone
as possible. Use the carcasses for soups and stews.*

Marinate the pheasant breasts in the oil, in a
dish covered with clingfilm, for about 1 hour.

To make the sauce, remove the flesh from the
mangoes and place in a food processor with the
lime juice. Purée and set aside. Whip the cream
until stiff, then fold in all the mango chutney
and 2 tablespoons of the mango purée. Place in
a saucepan, cover and refrigerate for about 1
hour.

Preheat the oven to Gas Mark 7/220°C/
425°F. In a frying-pan, heat the butter, then
brown the pheasant breasts all over (in two
batches) and transfer to a lightly buttered
baking sheet. Season lightly, then place in the
oven and bake for about 8 minutes, until just
cooked through. (Test by inserting a knife to
see whether the juices run clear.)

Meanwhile, remove the saucepan of mango
cream from the refrigerator and gently heat to a
simmer, stirring often, over a low heat for
about 10–15 minutes. Heat the remaining
mango purée in another saucepan over a gentle
heat and divide this equally among 8 warmed
plates. Place a pheasant breast over the purée
and top with a couple of spoons of the hot
creamy mango sauce. Garnish with slivers of
fresh mango and serve at once, with a mixture
of white and wild rice.

(pictured on pages 4/5)

PARMESAN CHICKEN DRUMSTICKS

Preparation time: 20 minutes + 45 minutes baking   Serves 8

75 g (3 oz) fresh parmesan
cheese, grated

50 g (2 oz) fresh
breadcrumbs

2 garlic cloves, crushed

grated zest of 1 large lemon

8 skinless chicken
drumsticks

50 g (2 oz) unsalted
butter, melted

salt and pepper

These chicken drumsticks are succulent and moist inside, and crunchy and full of flavour outside. The mixture of parmesan cheese, lemon and garlic is particularly savoury and, combined with freshly made breadcrumbs, it makes a delicious outer crust for the chicken. They can be served hot, warm or even cold, accompanied by a salad and some crusty bread. They are best eaten with fingers.

Preheat the oven to Gas Mark 6/200°C/400°F. In a bowl, blend together the cheese, breadcrumbs, garlic and lemon zest. Brush the chicken drumsticks all over with the melted butter, then coat them in the breadcrumb mixture. Press the crumbs well in.

Place the drumsticks on a buttered baking sheet, drizzle over any remaining butter and bake in the oven for about 45 minutes, until the coating is golden brown and the chicken cooked through.

CHICKEN BREAST WITH SPINACH AND TOMATO SAUCE

Preparation time: 20 minutes + 55 minutes cooking   Serves 4

For the tomato sauce:

500 g (1 lb) carton of
creamed tomatoes or 397 g
(14 oz) can of tomatoes,
sieved

1 garlic clove, crushed

1 onion, chopped finely

salt and pepper

This dish is simple, tasty and colourful. It needs only some sauté potatoes, french bread or a salad.

To make the tomato sauce, place all the ingredients in a large saucepan, cover and cook over a medium heat for about 20–25 minutes, until the onion is softened. Purée with a hand-held blender or in a food processor. Season to taste with salt and pepper.

Preheat the oven to Gas Mark 4/180°C/ 350°F. Dust the chicken breasts in the flour,

*Chicken Breast with Spinach and Tomato Sauce
Parmesan Chicken Drumsticks*

For the chicken and spinach:

4 boneless, skinless chicken breasts
1 tablespoon seasoned flour
25 g (1 oz) butter
250 g (8 oz) spinach, stalks removed
75 g (3 oz) mozzarella cheese, sliced thinly
salt and pepper

shaking off any excess. Quickly brown the chicken in the butter in a frying-pan. Transfer to an ovenproof dish and spoon over the tomato sauce.

Steam or microwave the spinach very briefly (about 1–2 minutes), drain well and season. Place the spinach over the tomato sauce, and the mozzarella slices over the spinach, then place the dish in the oven and bake for about 25–30 minutes, until the chicken is cooked and the mozzarella melted.

Serve piping hot, on warmed plates.

BOBOTIE

Preparation time: 15 minutes + 1 hour cooking   Serves 4

1 thick slice of white bread
125 ml (4 fl oz) milk
25 g (1 oz) butter
1 onion, chopped
1 garlic clove, chopped
500 g (1 lb) extra lean minced beef
1 tablespoon curry powder
1½ tablespoons apricot jam
1½ tablespoons wine vinegar
2 tablespoons raisins
2 eggs
salt and pepper

This recipe was given to me by a friend from South Africa, where Bobotie is an everyday dish. She also cooks a Fish Bobotie, using flaked white fish instead of mince. I love the sweet and savoury combination and the golden crust on the top. The classic accompaniments are boiled rice and a green salad or fruit chutneys.

Preheat the oven to Gas Mark 3/160°C/325°F. Soak the bread in half of the milk.

Heat the butter in a saucepan and brown the onion and garlic for about 5 minutes; add the minced beef, break it down and brown for another 5 minutes. Add the curry powder, jam, vinegar and raisins and cook for a couple of minutes. Finally, squeeze the bread out very gently, so that it remains moist, and add it to the mixture, with salt and pepper. If any milk remains from soaking the bread, then discard it. Combine well together, then turn into a 1-litre (1¾-pint) buttered ovenproof casserole or shallow dish.

Beat the eggs with the remaining milk, season with salt and pepper and then pour over the meat mixture. Bake at the top of the oven for about 50 minutes, or until set and golden.

PUDDINGS, BAKING AND PRESERVES

MILE-HIGH ICE CREAM PIE

Preparation time: 25 minutes + 1 hour chilling
+ 5 minutes baking + 20 minutes for the sauce   Serves 6–8

For the crust:

250 g (8 oz) digestive biscuits, crushed

75 g (3 oz) butter, melted

1.2 litres (2 pints) Cornish or vanilla dairy ice cream

For the meringue:

3 egg whites

6 tablespoons caster sugar

¼ teaspoon cream of tartar

½ teaspoon vanilla essence

For the hot fudge sauce:

125 g (4 oz) deluxe plain cooking chocolate

75 g (3 oz) unsalted butter

100 g (3½ oz) caster sugar

1 tablespoon cocoa powder

142 ml (¼ pint) carton of double cream

When I stayed with family friends in Bermuda one summer, I used to eat this very impressive dessert. It was made for a dinner party, and any leftovers were stored in the freezer for wayward day-time 'grazers', like myself, to snack on – my idea of heaven! If you have a large enough freezer, you can make double the quantity and then it really does look a mile high. I like to serve it with a hot fudge sauce, but it is also good with a purée of fresh berries such as strawberries or raspberries.

Mix the biscuit crumbs with the melted butter and press into a lightly buttered 20 cm (8-inch) flan tin. Leave to chill for about an hour.

Preheat the oven to Gas Mark 8/230°C/ 450°F. Soften the ice cream very slightly, then fill the biscuit shell with layers of the ice cream (do not press down too hard or the crust will break). Place in the freezer while you make the meringue.

To make the meringue, beat the egg whites until stiff, then gradually add the sugar, cream of tartar and vanilla. Cover the ice cream with the meringue, making sure that the edges are sealed. Place in the preheated oven for about 5 minutes, until lightly browned. (Watch it carefully; it can burn very quickly.)

Remove and cool as quickly as possible (before the ice cream starts to melt), then place in the freezer. Remove from the freezer about 20 minutes before serving with the sauce.

To make the sauce, melt the chocolate and butter in a double boiler or in a bowl set over simmering water. Add the sugar and cocoa and, over a low heat, whisk in the cream. Cook slowly for about 20 minutes, until thick and warm. (This can be made in advance and reheated in the microwave or in a double boiler.)

(pictured on pages 4/5)

CARAMEL AND PECAN ICE CREAM

Preparation time: 15 minutes + 2½ hours cooking
+ 2 hours chilling + 50 minutes freezing   Serves 4

397 g (14 oz) can of condensed milk

3 egg whites

a pinch of salt

284 ml (½ pint) carton of double cream, lightly whipped

3 tablespoons pecans, toasted lightly and chopped roughly

toasted pecan halves, to serve (optional)

Caramel is one of my favourite sweet tastes and I think it combines very well with nuts of all sorts – walnuts, hazelnuts, macadamias or pecans. Be sure to keep topping up the water simmering with the can of condensed milk, or there could be dire consequences!

Place the unopened can of condensed milk in a large saucepan of simmering water (the water should reach about three-quarters up the side of the can). Cover and cook for about 2½ hours, checking the water level every half hour.

Cool the unopened can at room temperature for a minimum of 2 hours (or keep it in the refrigerator overnight).

Whisk the egg whites with the salt until they form soft peaks. Open the can of milk and pour into the whipped cream; mix well, fold in the egg whites and add the pecans. Pour into an ice-cream machine and freeze for 45–50 minutes, until well churned. (If you do not have a machine, freeze in the coldest part of your freezer; beat the mixture well every half hour.)

Serve topped with the toasted pecans.

Caramel and Pecan Ice Cream
Mincemeat Ice Pie

MINCEMEAT ICE PIE

Preparation time: 20 minutes + 1 hour chilling
+ 1–2 hours freezing   Serves 6

200 g (7 oz) digestive or ginger biscuits, crushed

75 g (3 oz) butter, melted

250 g (8 oz) vegetarian or non-suet mincemeat

1–2 tablespoons rum or brandy

750 ml (1¼ pints) vanilla dairy ice-cream (not soft-scoop)

After Christmas, when I am left with yet another half-empty jar of mincemeat, I often use it in this simple, yet delicious, ice dessert. However, it is important that you use a vegetarian or non-suet variety as the mincemeat is uncooked in this recipe (mincemeat with suet tastes better if it is cooked). You can increase the amount of alcohol, depending on whether the guests are adults or children. Make sure you use a premium ice-cream – Cornish gives it a good golden colour. If you wish you can decorate the pie with a sprig of festive holly.

Line a 20 cm (8-inch) freezerproof flan dish with a sheet of clingfilm. Mix the biscuit crumbs and melted butter together, and press the mixture on to the base and up the sides of the flan dish. Refrigerate for about 1 hour.

Stir the rum or brandy into the mincemeat. Soften the ice cream a little, then mix together with the mincemeat. Spoon this mixture into the prepared flan dish, smooth the top and freeze until firm. (It takes 1–2 hours, depending on the quality of the ice cream.)

To serve, lift the pie out of the flan dish, using the clingfilm, and place on a plate.

CARROT AND SUNFLOWER SEED CAKE

Preparation time: 15 minutes
+ 1 hour baking   Makes 1 × 1 kg/2 lb cake

3 eggs, beaten

125 ml (4 fl oz) sunflower oil

1 teaspoon vanilla essence

200 g (7 oz) carrots, grated

This cake is moist, reasonably healthy and full of nutty texture. Unlike many carrot cake recipes, it requires no embellishments such as cream cheese icing, as it stands very well by itself.

Preheat the oven to Gas Mark 4/180°C/350°F. Grease a 1 kg (2 lb) loaf tin and line the base with baking parchment.

100 g (3½ oz) desiccated coconut	Beat the eggs with the oil and vanilla essence. Add the carrots, coconut, raisins and sunflower seeds; stir well together. Add the flour, salt, bicarbonate of soda, baking powder, cinnamon and sugar. Mix well to combine. Pour into the prepared loaf tin, pressing down to level the top. Bake in the oven for about 1 hour, until a skewer inserted in the centre, comes out clean. (After 30–40 minutes, cover loosely with foil, if becoming too brown.)
100 g (3½ oz) raisins	
100 g (3½ oz) sunflower seeds	
250 g (8 oz) plain wholemeal flour	
½ teaspoon salt	
1 teaspoon bicarbonate of soda	
1 teaspoon baking powder	Remove from the oven, cool in the tin for about 20 minutes, then turn out on to a wire rack to cool completely.
1 teaspoon cinnamon	
150 g (5 oz) soft brown sugar	

COCONUT FLAPJACKS

Preparation time: 15 minutes
+ 25 minutes baking

Makes about 24 bars

200 g (7 oz) margarine or butter

6 tablespoons golden syrup

25 g (1 oz) caster sugar

425 g (14 oz) porridge oats

75 g (3 oz) desiccated coconut

a pinch of salt

These are so quick to prepare and bake, you can rustle them up in a flash for unexpected guests. They freeze well and last for a couple of weeks in a biscuit tin, and are also ideal for the children's lunch boxes.

Preheat the oven to Gas Mark 4/180°C/350°F. Melt the margarine, syrup and sugar together in a saucepan. Add the oats, coconut and salt. Stir well to combine, then pour into a greased swiss–roll tin (23 × 33 cm/9 × 13 inches). Press down with the back of a spoon, then bake in the oven for about 25 minutes, until golden brown.

Cut into squares while still hot, and then leave to cool in the tin until cold. Lift out the flapjacks with a spatula and store in an airtight container.

GUGGY CAKE

Preparation time: 20 minutes + 30 minutes cooling
+ 1 hour baking

Makes 1 cake

150 g (5 oz) soft brown sugar	
150 g (5 oz) sultanas	
150 g (5 oz) currants	
250 ml (8 fl oz) water	
125 g (4 oz) butter or lard	
2 teaspoons mixed spice	
250 g (8 oz) self-raising flour, sifted	

This is a recipe my mother has used since the war, when lard was easier to obtain than butter. I have substituted butter for the lard, for a better depth of flavour. It is a great family favourite.

Mix together the sugar, sultanas, currants, water, butter and mixed spice in a saucepan. Heat very gently, until the butter melts, then leave to cool. Preheat the oven to Gas Mark 4/180°C/350°F.

Once the mixture is cold, stir in the sifted flour and combine well together. Pour into a buttered, base-lined loaf tin (1 kg/2 lb) and, bake in the oven for about 1 hour, or until a skewer inserted in the centre comes out clean. Wait until the cake is completely cold before turning out on to a wire rack. Serve in slices with or without butter.

STRAWBERRY AND COINTREAU JAM

Preparation time: 10 minutes + 1½ hours standing
+ 20 minutes cooking

Makes 3–4 × 500 g (1 lb) jars

1 kg (2 lb) fresh strawberries, hulled	
1 kg (2 lb) sugar with pectin	
zest of 1 orange	
7 g (¼ oz) unsalted butter	
2 tablespoons Cointreau	

Raspberry Jam with Drambuie
Strawberry and Cointreau Jam
Microwave Lemon Curd
Guggy Cake

Place the strawberries in a large saucepan or preserving pan, in layers with the sugar and orange zest. Leave to stand for 1 hour, stirring a couple of times.

Place the pan over a low heat until the sugar has dissolved. Bring to a full rolling boil, add the butter and boil rapidly for 4–5 minutes, or until setting point is reached. (Place some on a cold saucer; let it cool quickly and test with your finger to see whether it wrinkles – if so, it is ready). Remove from the heat, stir in the Cointreau and leave to stand for another 30 minutes. Pour into warmed, sterilised jars and leave to become completely cold before covering and storing in a dark, cool place.

MICROWAVE LEMON CURD

Preparation time: 30 minutes
+ 15 minutes cooking

Makes 3–4 × 500 g (1 lb) jars

250 g (8 oz) unsalted
butter

500 g (1 lb) granulated
sugar

350 ml (12 fl oz) lemon
juice

grated zest of 6–7 large
lemons

6 eggs, beaten and sieved

*Lemon curd is so versatile: it can be spread on toast,
bread or scones; it can make an ice cream, by mixing
with natural yogurt and freezing; it can be layered in
bread and butter pudding; or it can be mixed with
whipped cream and used to fill meringues or blackcurrant tarts. This recipe is my favourite, and it is the
only time I use the microwave for cooking as opposed
to reheating. The important thing to remember is to
check every minute and whisk frequently.*

Place the butter, sugar, lemon juice and zest in a
large microwave-proof bowl. Cook uncovered
on High for 3–5 minutes, until the butter has
completely melted and the sugar has
completely dissolved; stir every minute.

Cool for 2–3 minutes, then whisk in the
beaten eggs gradually. Cook uncovered on
High for about 5–8 minutes, checking and
whisking every minute. Remove once the curd
has thickened. (It should not be too solid, as it
will thicken on cooling – aim for the
consistency of lightly whipped cream.) Pour
into warmed, sterilised jars, tap the base of the
jars to level the surface, and cover only when
completely cold. It will keep in the fridge for
up to 6 weeks.

RASPBERRY JAM WITH DRAMBUIE

Preparation time: 10 minutes
+ 50 minutes cooking

Makes 3 × 500 g (1 lb) jars

1 kg (2 lb) fresh
raspberries

1 kg (2 lb) preserving or
granulated sugar

15 g (½ oz) butter

1 tablespoon Drambuie

*Raspberry jam has great childhood memories for me –
picking the raspberries into bowls in the garden, then
waiting for the sweet heady smell of jam to waft from
the kitchen. For me, the best jam has always been
freshly made, as it has such a vivid colour and the
taste of the berries is so intense. It can also be made
with well-drained frozen raspberries. The addition of*

Drambuie makes this recipe rather more suitable for adults, and it makes a splendid gift, with a decoration of tartan ribbon.

Place the raspberries in a large saucepan or preserving pan and simmer very gently for about 20 minutes in their own juices until soft.

Add the sugar, and, stirring constantly, heat gently until the sugar has dissolved.

Add the butter, bring to the boil and boil rapidly for 25–30 minutes, or until setting point is reached (see Strawberry and Cointreau Jam, page 84). Remove the pan from the heat, stir in the Drambuie and pot at once in warm sterilised jars (taking great care; it is very hot!). Cover when completely cold, and store in a cool, dark place.

DOUBLE CHOCOLATE CHIP COOKIES

Preparation time: 20 minutes
+ 12–15 minutes baking

Makes about 24

250 g (8 oz) golden caster sugar

250 g (8 oz) unsalted butter

2 large egg yolks (size 1–2)

250 g (8 oz) plain flour, sifted

½ teaspoon salt

50 g (2 oz) walnut pieces

115 g (4 oz) packet of milk chocolate drops

115 g (4 oz) packet of plain chocolate drops

These American-style cookies are bulging with chocolate drops and nuts. The outside is crunchy, while the inside should be slightly soft and chewy. Ring the changes with the chocolate drops – I use a mixture of plain and milk, but if you can find white chocolate or butterscotch, these are also delicious. Vary the type of nuts used too – a combination of unsalted peanuts and pecans or macadamias is good. Although these freeze well, mine have only very seldom reached the freezer – they are a great family favourite.

Preheat the oven to Gas Mark 4/180°C/350°F. Place the sugar, butter and egg yolks in a bowl and beat together. Add the flour, salt and nuts and mix until just combined. Stir in the chocolate drops.

Place spoonfuls of the mixture on to 2 or 3 lightly greased baking sheets, leaving a little space between them. Flatten them down slightly with your fingers.

87

Bake in the oven for about 12–15 minutes, until they are still slightly soft to the touch.

Leave the cookies on the baking sheets for about 2 minutes, then transfer to a wire rack and cool completely before storing in airtight containers.

BLACKCURRANT MINT CRUMBLE CAKE

Preparation time: 40 minutes + 20 minutes chilling
+ 50 minutes baking + 20 minutes cooling   Serves 8–10

For the base:

375 g (12 oz) plain flour, sifted

1 tablespoon caster sugar

250 g (8 oz) butter, chopped

2 egg yolks

1 tablespoon lemon juice

For the filling:

1 tablespoon plain flour

2 egg whites

500 g (1 lb) blackcurrants

2 tablespoons chopped fresh mint

For the crumble:

150 g (5 oz) plain flour, sifted

200 g (7 oz) caster sugar

125 g (4 oz) butter, chopped

This is more of a pudding – to be served warm with cream or greek-style yogurt – than a cake, although it is also very good cold, with a cup of tea or coffee. If you are using frozen fruit, be sure that it is well defrosted and drained, or the base will become soggy. Blueberries are a good substitute for the blackcurrants.

To make the base, butter a swiss-roll tin (23 × 33 cm/9 × 13 inches). Mix the flour and sugar in a bowl, then rub in the butter until the mixture resembles breadcrumbs. Add the egg yolks and lemon juice and mix together to form a ball. (Add a couple of drops of extra juice if necessary.) Chill for 20 minutes, then press the mixture into the prepared tin. Preheat the oven to Gas Mark 6/200°C/400°F.

To make the filling, sieve the flour over the base (this prevents the juices from the fruit seeping into the base). Whisk the egg whites until stiff, and carefully fold in the blackcurrants and mint, then spread this over the base.

To make the crumble, mix the flour and sugar together, then rub in the butter until crumbly. Spoon over the blackcurrants, pressing down gently. Bake in the centre of the oven for 45–50 minutes, or until the top is golden and the blackcurrant juices are just beginning to seep out.

Leave to cool for about 20 minutes, before cutting into slices and serving warm or cold.

Toffee Oat Squares
Blackcurrant Mint
Crumble Cake

TOFFEE OAT SQUARES

Preparation time: 15 minutes + 15 minutes cooking
+ 20 minutes baking + 1–2 hours cooling   Makes about 20–24

250 g (8 oz) plain flour, sifted

125 g (4 oz) porridge oats

175 g (6 oz) light-brown muscovado sugar

½ teaspoon bicarbonate of soda

¼ teaspoon salt

175 g (6 oz) unsalted butter, chopped

250 g (8 oz) deluxe plain cooking chocolate

142 ml (¼ pint) carton of double cream

2 × 227 g (7½ oz) bags of Devon toffees

These are wickedly rich and decadently extravagant, yet I challenge anyone to stop at just one square – they are so moreish. The only problem with this recipe is having to wait for up to 2 hours, while the toffee sets, before sampling!

Preheat the oven to Gas Mark 4/180°C/350°F. Place the flour, oats, sugar, bicarbonate of soda and salt in a food processor and process briefly to form crumbs. Add the butter and process until the mixture just starts to stick together. Grease a swiss-roll tin (23 × 33 cm/9 × 13 inches) and press three-quarters of the mixture into the base of the tin. Melt the chocolate in a bowl placed over a pan of very hot water and pour over the top. Spread evenly and allow the chocolate to harden by placing the tin in the refrigerator.

Bring the cream to the boil, in a heavy saucepan, then lower the heat to a simmer. Add the toffees, and stir until melted and smooth (about 10–15 minutes).

Pour the toffee mixture evenly over the chocolate, and then sprinkle the remaining oat mixture over the top, rather like a crumble topping. Place on a baking sheet and bake in the oven for about 20 minutes, or until the edges are golden brown. Cut around the edges of the tin, to loosen, then cool completely before cutting into squares. Allow to cool for a couple of hours (or 1 hour in the refrigerator), so that the toffee hardens sufficiently.

CHOCOLATE AND MINT MOUSSE

Preparation time: 30 minutes + 2–3 hours chilling   Serves 6

250 g (8 oz) deluxe plain
cooking chocolate

50 g (2 oz) unsalted butter

1 tablespoon crème de
menthe

4 large eggs (size 2),
separated

8 large mint leaves,
chopped very finely

fresh mint leaves, to
garnish

pouring cream, to serve

The combination of chocolate with mint is so often eaten in chocolates and mint creams, but rarely combined in desserts. Using fresh mint as well as a mint liqueur means a greater depth of flavour. Make sure the mint you use is spearmint or another smooth-leafed mint. Some mint leaves, such as Apple or Bowles mint, are rather 'hairy' and do nothing for the texture of this delectable mousse! It should be eaten the same day.

Melt the chocolate, butter and crème de menthe together (in a microwave on Medium, or in a double boiler). Cool slightly, then add the beaten egg yolks. Mix well, and add the chopped mint. Whisk the egg whites until stiff, then fold into the mixture; combine well, but not too vigorously. Pour it into a glass bowl or individual ramekins. Chill for 2–3 hours, then decorate with fresh mint and serve with cream.

BORDER TART

Preparation time: 25 minutes + 1½ hours chilling
+ 10 minutes for 'blind' baking + 35 minutes baking
+ 1 hour cooling   Makes 1 tart

**For the shortcrust pastry
case:**

250 g (8 oz) plain flour,
sifted

150 g (5 oz) unsalted
butter, cubed

2 teaspoons caster sugar

1 egg yolk

1–2 tablespoons cold water

For the filling:

50 g (2 oz) butter

This is my version of the tart which originates in the Borders area of Scotland. The authentic recipe calls for an enriched yeast pastry case, filled with almonds, peel and marzipan. My version is an Edinburgh variation, using a shortcrust base.

To make the pastry case, place the flour, butter and sugar in a food processor or bowl and combine together until the mixture resembles breadcrumbs. Add the egg yolk and sufficient water for the pastry to come together in a ball. Cover with clingfilm and chill for 30 minutes. Roll the pastry out to fit a 20 cm (8-inch) flan tin and chill for 1 hour.

50 g (2 oz) soft dark brown sugar
2 eggs, beaten
275 g (9 oz) raisins
grated zest of 1 large lemon
For the glacé icing:
1–2 tablespoons icing sugar, sifted
1–2 teaspoons cold water

Cream the butter with the sugar, then add the eggs, raisins and lemon zest.

Prick the base of the tart and bake blind for 10 minutes (with baking parchment and beans) at Gas Mark 6/200°C/400°F. Remove the baking parchment and beans, then cool slightly. Reduce the oven to Gas Mark 5/190°C/375°F.

Pour the mixture into the pastry case and bake in the oven for 30–35 minutes, until golden brown. Remove from the oven and allow to cool.

To make the glacé icing, mix the icing sugar with sufficient water to make a runny consistency. Drizzle or pipe strips of glacé icing across the tart, once it is completely cold.

WALNUT AND PINE KERNEL BREAD

Preparation time: 15 minutes + 1½ hours proving/rising + 25 minutes baking

Makes 2 loaves

25 g (1 oz) fresh yeast (or 15 g/½ oz dried yeast)
½ teaspoon caster sugar
275 ml (9 fl oz) tepid water
125 g (4 oz) Granary® flour
375 g (12 oz) strong white bread flour
1 teaspoon salt
2 teaspoons walnut oil
25 g (1 oz) unsalted butter, cubed
50 g (2 oz) walnut pieces
50 g (2 oz) pine kernels
1 egg yolk, to brush

I love to serve this bread with cheese, as it has a lovely savoury, nutty flavour. It freezes beautifully; when completely thawed, it should be warmed in foil in a warm oven for about 15 minutes.

Place the yeast in a small bowl with the sugar and about 100 ml/3½ fl oz of the tepid water (test with your little finger – it should feel warm, not hot). Mash with a fork (if you are using fresh yeast), stir well and leave for about 5 minutes in a warm place until it froths a little.

Place the flours, salt, 1 teaspoon of the walnut oil and the butter in a bowl and rub together until it resembles breadcrumbs. Once the yeast is frothy, pour it into the bowl, with the remaining tepid water. Mix until the dough begins to form a ball.

Oil a bowl with the remaining walnut oil, place the dough in it. Cover with a damp tea towel and put it in a warm place for about 1 hour, or until it has doubled in size.

Preheat the oven to Gas Mark 7/220°C/ 425°F. On a lightly floured surface, knead the walnuts and pine kernels into the dough, then cut into two and roll into 'sausage' shapes about 25–30 cm (10–12 inches) in length. Place on an oiled baking sheet, well spaced from each other. Cover with a damp tea towel and put in a warm place for another 30 minutes or so, until the loaves have doubled in size.

Brush the tops with beaten egg and bake in the oven for about 25 minutes, until golden brown. To test, tap the bottom of the loaf – it should sound hollow.

Remove and cool on a wire rack.

CLOUTIE DUMPLING

Preparation time: 30 minutes + 4 hours cooking   Serves 8

250 g (8 oz) plain flour, sifted

200 g (7 oz) sugar

1 teaspoon cinnamon

1 teaspoon mixed spice

125 g (4 oz) suet

125 g (4 oz) sultanas

125 g (4 oz) currants

125 g (4 oz) dates, chopped

1 teaspoon baking soda

200 ml (7 fl oz) water, cold tea or sour milk

caster sugar

custard, cream or crème fraîche, to serve

My aunt makes this Cloutie Dumpling on family birthdays, a tradition in my home town of Dundee. Everyone has their own individual recipes (most unwritten), but this one is more or less my grandmother's (give or take a pinch of this and a handful of that). It can be cooked in a greased pudding basin, but there will be no characteristic 'skin'; so, for authenticity, it should be boiled in a cloth, since 'cloutie' is the Scots' word for cloth.

Mix the flour, sugar, cinnamon, mixed spice, suet, sultanas, currants, dates and baking soda together with sufficient water (or cold tea, or sour milk) to make a soft dough of stiff, dropping consistency.

Dip a large pudding cloth (or a clean tea towel) into boiling water; drain well, and lay out flat on a table. Sprinkle flour and then sugar lightly over the cloth (this forms the characteristic skin). Place the mixture on to the cloth. Tie securely with string, allowing a little room for expansion, and place on a heatproof plate in the bottom of a large saucepan. Pour in enough boiling water to cover, then simmer for 4 hours.

Turn out carefully on to an ovenproof serving plate (if you dip it quickly into cold water, the skin should not stick to the cloth). Dry the dumpling off in the oven, for about 10 minutes. Sprinkle with some caster sugar and serve with custard, cream or crème fraîche.

GINGER MILLIONAIRE'S SHORTBREAD

Preparation time: 20 minutes
+ 10 minutes cooking + 1½ hours cooling   Makes about 24 squares

For the base:

250 g (8 oz) digestive biscuits, crushed

125 g (4 oz) gingersnap biscuits, crushed

150 g (5 oz) unsalted butter, melted

For the caramel:

397 g (14 oz) can of condensed milk

175 g (6 oz) unsalted butter

175 g (6 oz) caster sugar

1½ tablespoons ginger syrup (from a jar of stem ginger)

For the topping:

250 g (8 oz) deluxe plain cooking chocolate

In Dundee, after children had been swimming, they had some sort of treat – called, rather appropriately, a 'Shivery Bite': a piece of millionaire's shortbread was perfect to lure children out of the water, for few can resist it. I have introduced one of my favourite spices, ginger, to the traditional recipe, as I think it enhances the caramel flavour.

Combine the biscuit crumbs with the butter. Press into the base of a greased swiss-roll tin (23 × 33 cm/9 × 13 inches) and chill in the refrigerator.

Meanwhile place the condensed milk in a heavy-based saucepan with the other caramel ingredients and, over a low heat, stir until the sugar has dissolved. Bring the mixture to the boil, whisking or beating continuously (watch it does not burn) for about 5 minutes. (By this time, it will be a golden brown colour.) Remove from the heat and beat vigorously for another 2 minutes, then pour it over the biscuit base and leave to cool completely.

Once it is cold, melt the chocolate in a bowl placed over a pan of very hot water, and pour over; allow to cool (about 1 hour) before cutting into squares.

INDEX TO RECIPES

Cover design: Moore Lowenhoff
Text design: Ken Vail Graphic Design
Photography: Jess Koppel
Styling: Marian Price
Food preparation for photography: Mandy Wagstaff
Cover illustration: Sally Swabey
Line illustrations: John Woodcock
Typesetting: Goodfellow & Egan, Cambridge